D0933387

WOMEN
WHO DATE TOO MUCH

*...and Those
Who Should
Be So Lucky*

WITHDRAWN

OTHER BOOKS BY LINDA SUNSHINE

She's Just THAT Into You!

All Things Alice

All Things Oz

The Family Dog

The Family Dinner

Waiting for My Baby

Our Grandmothers

A Passion for Shoes

The Illustrated Woody Allen Reader

Dating Iron John

Lovers

How NOT to Turn into Your Mother

"Mom Loves Me Best" and Other Lies You Told Your Sister

The Memoirs of Bambi Goldbloom: Growing Up in New Jersey

Plain Jane Works Out

WITHDRAWN

WOMEN
WHO DATE TOO MUCH

...and Those Who Should Be So Lucky

Happy Dating, Great Sex, Healthy Relationships, and Other Delusions

Linda Sunshine

THREE RIVERS PRESS
NEW YORK

Copyright © 1988, 2005 by Linda Sunshine

All rights reserved.

Published in the United States by Three Rivers Press, an imprint of the
Crown Publishing Group, a division of Random House, Inc., New York.

www.crownpublishing.com

Three Rivers Press and the Tugboat design are registered trademarks of
Random House, Inc.

Originally published in different form in hardcover in the United States
by New American Library, New York, in 1988.

"Sex Ruins Everything" was originally published in *New York Woman,*
July 1991.

"25 Snappy Comebacks to 'Why Aren't You Married Yet?'" was originally
published in *Woman,* March 1990.

Library of Congress Cataloging-in-Publication Data
Sunshine, Linda.
Women who date too much—and those who should be so lucky: happy
dating, great sex, healthy relationships, and other delusions/Linda
Sunshine.
1. Dating (Social customs)—Anecdotes.   2. Single women—United
States—Psychology—Anecdotes.   3. Mate selection—United States—
Anecdotes.   4. Interpersonal relations—Anecdotes.   I. Title.
HQ801.S94   2005
646.7'7—dc22   2004025270

ISBN 1-4000-9817-3

Printed in the United States of America

Design by Jan Derevjanik and Jennifer Beal

10   9   8   7   6   5   4   3   2   1

First Edition

*This is dedicated to the one I love,
the one I loved and lost, the one my mom
wanted me to love, the one who loved me,
the one I liked but could not love, and the
ones who stuck around anyway.*

contents

CLARK GABLE
IN
No Man of Her Own
WITH
CAROLE LOMBARD and
DOROTHY MACKAIL
DIRECTED BY WESLEY RUGGLES
FROM STORY BY EDMUND GOULDING
and BENJAMIN GLAZER
a

you can't hurry love,
you just have to date!

preface

You need somebody to love while you
are looking for somebody to love.

SHELAGH DELANEY,
A TASTE OF HONEY, 1958

Some of us are becoming the men
we wanted to marry.

GLORIA STEINEM

How I Came to Write This Book

IT WAS THE AFTERNOON OF DECEMBER 31. I was sitting at home waiting for my new boyfriend to call. His name wasn't Jim, but that's what I'll call him.[1]

Jim was as close to perfection as I'd found, although, truthfully, I had to admit, I didn't know him very well. Yet Jim had passed the "S" test: he was single, straight, successful, and sexy, which was as close to a miracle as one could expect these days.

Jim and I had met three weeks before. We'd had four dates. I was trying hard not to rush things, although I had already selected a name for our firstborn.

I was relatively certain Jim would ask me out for New Year's Eve even though he had only about eight hours left until midnight struck. I kept reminding myself to give Jim the benefit of the doubt, and that eight hours was almost enough time for me to get dressed, especially since I had purchased the perfect New Year's Eve Prada dress just after our first phone conversation.

The phone rang and I ran to answer it. It was my agent, Beulah.

I tried not to sound disappointed as I listened to Beulah explain that she'd just come from lunch with a publisher who wanted a writer for a humorous book about dating. Would I consider the project?

I told her I was expecting an important call and couldn't talk, but I'd think about the idea.

"Great," she said. "I've set up a meeting the day after tomorrow to discuss the book. This project will be great for your career!"

---

1. His name was Joel Aaron Fargoet, 745 East 83rd Street, Apt. 2L, New York, New York 10028. Age: 42. Height: 6 feet. Weight: 173. Shirt size: $15^{1}/_{2}$, 34. Social Security Number: 151-39-9695. ATM password: Mama.

I agreed to take the meeting and hung up the phone. Thinking about dating, I realized I was something of an expert on the subject, considering I had almost twenty years of combat training in the field, so to speak. The thought made me depressed, which made me hungry. I checked my voice mail to make sure my outgoing message was appropriately perky and that I sounded like someone who had a great life, though I was not quite sure what someone with a great life sounded like. (I've never had a conversation with Jennifer Aniston.) I grabbed my cell phone, just in case Jim remembered that number and ran to the deli across the street. (Even important calls can wait for take-out.)

At the counter, I said hello to Siros, the guy who handled take-out orders, asked for my usual chicken salad on rye, light on the mayo, and eavesdropped on the conversation between two young women sitting at the counter.

"New Year's Eve just ain't a holiday for singles," sighed the woman with a head of hair that looked like it was styled by a Cuisinart (speed setting: Pulverize).

"It ain't so great if you're married, either," said her companion, a poor soul who had obviously never learned how to operate a tweezer. "I mean, you stare across the table at this *person* and you wonder—how'd I get stuck with *him* for another year?"

"New Year's is only good if you've just met someone and you're falling in love," Siros piped in, and the two women nodded their heads in agreement.

I thought about Jim and felt rather smug. Sandwich in hand, I rushed back to the apartment. The phone was ringing.

It's him!

We chitchat for a few minutes before Jim gets down to business. He's calling, he says, to tell me he's gotten involved with another woman and, as a one-woman guy, he feels guilty about us. He says he doesn't think we should see each other anymore.

I want to ask him how he had time to get involved with another woman while he was dating me but, even in my desperate state of panic, I know this is a stupid question. Instead, I ask, "Does this mean you're not asking me for New Year's?"

"I guess not. I already have a date tonight," he informs me.

"With who?"

"With this other woman, the one I'm telling you about. She's a doctor. We met three months ago in a chat room for singles with small pets."

"You don't have a small pet," I protest.

"Neither does she." He laughs as if I just made a joke.

"Well fine, then," I say, summoning up my last ounce of dignity. "I could tell you I hope it'll work out but I'd be lying. So, good-bye and have a nice life."

"Gee, you make it sound so final," he says.

"It is."

"We'll run into each other again."

Yes, and I hope I am driving a Mack truck when we do, I want to say. Instead I offer this feeble attempt at a zinger, "Not if I can help it."

I slam down the phone and have a long, long cry in between bites of my chicken salad on rye. I take a long bath. I watch forty-seven reruns of *It's a Wonderful Life*. I make myself a cup of tea. I eat everything in the kitchen, including a small jar of mayonnaise.

I make sure I am sleeping by midnight and that I remain as unconscious as possible for as long as possible.

When I surface, two days later, my eyes are still puffy, my nose is stuffed, my stomach is bloated, and my fingers and toes have shriveled into prunes after being submerged in the bath for so long. I don't think I could feel any worse. Then I realize I have to get dressed and go to a meeting where I am expected not only to be bright and chipper but to make jokes about being single. This is the story of my life, I think, as I pull the covers over my head.

Eventually, I get out of bed and walk into the kitchen to make a cup of coffee, where I notice Jim's business card tacked on my bulletin board. I rip it to shreds. Then I stick my head out of the window. "What's funny about dating?" I scream to the world.

"Absolutely nothing!" responds a young woman walking her dog on Sixth Avenue.

Two hours later, I'm in the publisher's office with my agent. I am dressed all in black (trying to disguise the fifteen pounds I gained over the weekend) and wearing sunglasses to hide my puffy eyes. I can barely speak. Luckily, my agent is being bright and chipper and making jokes.

I'm sulking. I am thinking about Jim, rewording in my mind our conversation so that I sound like the one who's dumping him. It's a stretch, I have to admit, even for someone who, as my shrink once said, "has an amazing capacity to rewrite her own personal history."

The publisher nods at me. "So, are you interested in our idea?" he asks with a smile.

"Can I write a chapter on revenge?" I inquire.

"Why not?" he shrugs.

"On holding a grudge?"

"Uh, I suppose."

"On being celibate?"

My agent kicks me under the table.

The publisher scratches his head. "We are talking about a *humor* book, right?"

Beulah laughs flirtatiously in that way that always makes me want to strangle her. "She's just kidding. Really."

I wasn't, of course, but never mind.

My friend Mary, the part-time astrologer, says, "There's a gift in everything." And, I guess the gift here is that I get to write a book and make a profit off Jim and all the other guys who've inadvertently provided me with material for this book.

Fine, but just don't ask me if I'd trade the book, the contract, and my agent for a date with Jim.

Excuse me, but I've got to go get something to eat.

> Linda Sunshine
> Friday afternoon in March
> Burger King, New York City

National
ctures inc.
Presents
Flirting with Lo
WITH
Colleen Moor
AND
Conway Tear
Adapted from LeROY SCOTT'S great novel "COUNTERF
Directed by JOHN FRANCIS DILLON
First National Pi

the history of

dating

Time is nature's way of keeping
everything from happening
all at once.

UNKNOWN

No one should have to dance
backwards all their lives.

JILL RUCKELSHAUS,
NEW YORK TIMES,
AUGUST 3, 1973

the wedding march of civilization

dating from adam and eve to ben and 2 jens

Mankind's first official attempt at dating took place in the Garden of Eden, and, like most dates, it was based on a profound misunderstanding.

Adam was eating breakfast one morning when he spied a young woman staring at him from behind a rubber tree. Upon closer inspection, Adam thought he detected a certain hungry look in this strange creature's eyes, so he kindly offered her a piece of his fruit. "Wanna date?" Adam asked.

Eve, the original single woman, heard opportunity knocking loud and clear. "You bet," she said. "Let's do lunch." And she rushed off to wash her hair.

Historians note that the phenomenon of dating might've been radically altered if Adam had been eating a grapefruit that fateful morning.

But he wasn't, and, as we know, Adam and Eve continued to "date"—on and off—for the remainder of their lives, which wasn't all that difficult considering Eve had virtually no competition in Eden and millions of years would pass before the discovery of cellulite. A noted historian has also pointed out that Eve had one great advantage over all the rest of her sex because, in his wildest moments of rage, Adam could never accuse Eve of being just like her mother.

Throughout the Ages we now call Stone, Ice, Bronze, and Iron, dating consisted mainly of informal gatherings for the purpose of hunting and foraging (sort of like the club scene in bare feet and a fur coat). Romance during this time was minimal, since primitive man had yet to create computer dating. In fact, nothing much happened until the scientific discovery of astrology, which altered the course of dating by enabling single men to introduce themselves by asking: "What's your sign?"

The next momentous event in dating history is credited to Cleopatra, the Queen of Egypt. After her boyfriend, Caesar, was assassinated, Cleo began fooling around with Marcus Antonius, her best friend's husband. Thus, Cleopatra became the first woman in recorded history to date a married man. Like many such relationships, this one ended badly. Cleopatra committed suicide at age thirty-nine.

Centuries passed and dating took a backseat to lots and lots of wars—at least until the French Revolution, when things picked up, thanks to Marie Antoinette. A genuine boy toy, Marie liked to mix heavy necking and whipped cream, a combination that greatly aroused Louis XVI and, more importantly, was the method by which the couple inadvertently invented French kissing. Unbeknownst to Louis, Marie demonstrated their discovery to almost every garçon at Versailles, which is probably why dating enjoyed a healthy revival in the late 1700s.

During the 1800s, several technological advances radically altered the course of dating. In 1824, the process of binding rubber to cloth was first patented. This seemingly innocuous event would subsequently lead to the invention of the girdle, a garment that almost single-handedly wiped dating off the face of the earth.

In 1864, George Pullman built his first railway sleeping car, thereby creating a reason to take a date along on a business trip. It wasn't long before people began making out in other moving vehicles as well. In fact, Pullman's early efforts probably account for the popularity of airplane bathrooms among today's traveling singles (hence the evolution of the Mile High Club, of which I am not a member—not yet at least).

In 1867, the typewriter was invented, which didn't directly affect dating per se but did permit me to write this sentence without using quill and ink.

No one would dispute that the most momentous—and time-saving—contribution to dating took place in 1891 with the invention of the zipper.

In 1907, the Model T Ford was mass-produced for the first time, enabling everyone to own a car. This was important, because how else could people get to the drive-in?

What is disputed, however, is the exact moment in history when the word *relationship* crept into our dating vocabulary. Attempting to discover the origin of this term, researchers have studied hundreds of hours of reality dating shows, but all to no avail.

Scholars have noted, coincidentally, that their inability to determine when a "date" became a "relationship" is the same dilemma that confuses most single men today.

Yet no discussion of dating would be complete without evaluating, in some detail, the seminal singles book of our century, *Sex and the Single Girl,* which was published in May 1963 and, almost instantly, became one of the most talked about books of its time. Reviewed extensively, the intrinsic intellectual value of this book was perhaps best described by Miss Joan Crawford, who stated: "It [this book] should be on every man's bed table—when he's free, that is." (For further information about how Helen Gurley Brown boosted the social life of the unavailable man, see Dating Married Men on page 127.) As proof of its relevance to modern-day society, *Sex and the Single Girl* was made into a movie starring Tony Curtis and Natalie Wood.

In the following paragraph from her book, Mrs. Brown displays a remarkable talent for deep psychological insight into the inner workings of the male psyche. "When a man thinks of a single woman," she writes, "he pictures her alone in her apartment, smooth legs sheathed in pink silk Capri pants, lying tantalizingly among dozens of satin cushions, trying to read but not very successfully, for *he* is in that room—filling her thoughts, her dreams, her life."

While parts of *Sex and the Single Girl* have become somewhat dated (Who can afford to live alone anymore? Who has smooth legs?), a great deal of the book, particularly Mrs. Brown's sound advice, has remained, surprisingly, as refreshingly and frankly applicable to today's single gal as it was for the swinging sixties gal of long ago. Take, for instance, the following examples of Helen Gurley Brown's wisdom:

- There are three kinds of people you absolutely must have in your single life: a really good butcher, a crack car mechanic, and a rich and powerful married couple.

- Demand and inspire expensive gifts from your dates. These are the rewards of single life.

- If he asks to go Dutch treat on your date, don't stand on ceremony. Dump him immediately.

As for me, my favorite piece of advice from *Sex and the Single Girl* involves not sex, but office politics. Over and over, Mrs. Brown stresses the importance of having a solid career and competing in the marketplace on an equal footing with men. In this way, perhaps Mrs. Brown could be considered a forerunner of the feminist movement. Take, for example, the following piece of advice, which most certainly helped Gloria Steinem (and others like her) catapult up the corporate ladder. "About every six weeks several girls from my office and I round up all our clothes that need altering, and we gossip and sew for the evening. Isn't that jolly?"

While this idea strikes me as a wonderful way to finally fix those loose buttons on my raincoat, when I worked in corporate publishing, the other female executives in my office were never very receptive to the suggestion. Even when I brought my dog-eared copy of *Sex and the Single Girl* to the office, no one was even remotely interested in a jolly evening of sewing and girl talk.

The decline in the popularity of sewing circles among female co-workers is, perhaps, not the only difference in the social life of a single woman in the days of *Sex and the Single Girl* and today. If someone were writing a twenty-first-century version of Helen Gurley Brown's opus (and I'm applying for the job), she might have to title the book *Sex and the Insignificant Other*.

In other scholarly endeavors, researchers have studied the two most popular sex books of the past few decades in order to examine the sexual preferences of modern times. In the early 1970s, millions of copies of *Everything You Always Wanted to Know About Sex But Were Afraid to Ask* were sold; in the late 1970s, the best-selling book was entitled *The Joy of Sex*. We can deduce from these facts that, as we moved into the latter part of that decade, people preferred books with shorter titles.

In the 1980s, many scholars maintained that the quintessential description of modern dating patterns could be found in the seminal singles movie *The Big Chill*, more specifically in Meg's (Mary Kay Place) speech after we learn that Nick (William Hurt) isn't going to father her child. (A fact that would depress the hell out of any single gal.)

"They're either married or gay," Meg observes about the men in her life. "And if they're not gay, they've just broken up with the most wonderful woman in the world or they've just broken up with a bitch who looks exactly like me. They're in transition from a monogamous relationship and they need more space or they're tired of space but they just can't commit or they want to commit but they're afraid to get close. They want to get close and you don't want to get near them."

It is interesting to note that Meg's speech was validated by a landmark Harvard survey in the 1980s which concluded that women in their late thirties and early forties had about as much chance of getting married as they did of winning the New York State Lottery twice in a row. In a more recent study, researchers at Stanford linked the enormous media attention that this survey generated to the tremendous rise of Prozac in the latter part of the twentieth century.

In the past twenty years, statisticians note that modern dating problems are exacerbated by the fact that there are lots more single women than single men in today's dating pool.

To illustrate the point, the chart on page 23 details the ratio of single men to single women in New York City. (Manhattan is considered a Mecca for singles, being one of the few cities in the country where, traditionally, bars stay open almost until dawn, Chinese take-out is available 24/7, and shrinks are on call eleven months a year.)

The figures in our chart were compiled by the Singles Census Bureau, which is a group also known as Anxious Mothers of Single Daughters in Manhattan (AMOSDIM), which tracks the number of available straight single men and holds a formal retirement ceremony every time one of them marries or moves to Florida.

Experts report that the reasons for the increasing number of single women in the early 2000s are psychological, social, and demographic and include the following:

- Many women are working at good jobs and supporting themselves. However, because women's salaries are still well below men's, economics does play an important factor in women's decisions to remain single. Because of their comparatively limited incomes, women are hesitant to get married and take on the additional financial burden of supporting a husband and, perhaps, children.

- Men classified as unmarried by the Census Bureau are often not interested in getting married, even when women spend a fortune on leg-waxing and expensive perfume. In fact, many of these men prefer to reserve the leg-waxing appointments for themselves.

- Many single women in their thirties and forties are attracted only to unavailable men, spending a good deal of their potentially marriageable years in love with their married bosses or psychiatrists. Thus, these women have greatly decreased their chances of ever finding a companion to join them in the matrimonial state.

- Many of our mothers, born in the baby-boom years, had the misfortune of entering their early to mid-twenties at a very critical moment in American history. Specifically, these women came of marriageable age during the first broadcasts of *The Mary Tyler Moore Show*. The enormous popularity of the show encouraged these women to stay home on Saturday night and watch television instead of going out on blind dates, thus greatly decreasing their chances of snagging a husband. In addition, these women were brainwashed by the blatant propaganda promoted by the show, namely that it was okay to be single, as long as you were really skinny, dressed well, and had funny friends. It wasn't until these baby boomers hit their late thirties and early forties that it dawned on them that Mary Tyler Moore, in real life, was married to a successful Jewish doctor sixteen years her junior. Many women have never fully recovered from this crushing revelation and they have passed their phobias on to their daughters who, by no coincidence I suppose, grew up on *Sex and the City*, a show that essentially promoted the same propaganda as Mary but, okay, with a 2000 spin. As Carrie Bradshaw would surely conclude, it's okay to be single as long as you are really skinny, well dressed, have funny friends, and discuss oral sex six times a day.

Today's single women are a breed apart from the single gals of Helen Gurley Brown's generation. No longer known as Jolly Spinsters, the modern single woman is likely to own her own co-op or condo and to have learned not to feel out of place with her married friends and relatives. These women usually have a good relationship with children, either their friends' or siblings'. They travel frequently and are well informed, politically active, and health conscious. Often they have challenging jobs and many social advantages. Their lives are wholly successful even though the vast majority of them are unbelievably depressed most of the time.

In order to get a firsthand account of the dating scene and how it affects the modern woman, this reporter recently attended a gathering of single women who congregated at the Dew Drop Inn in Massapequa, New York, to discuss their social lives with the media. The room was filled to capacity with unmarried women, all of whom wore T-shirts that read: "I'd rather be married, or at least dating someone special." In the crowded room, this reporter noted that the ticking of biological clocks was almost deafening.

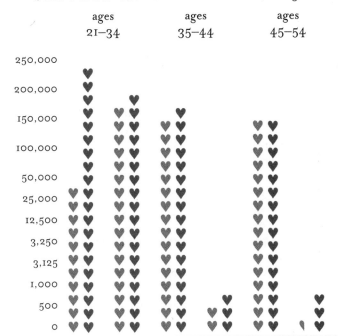

♥ = Population of singles in New York City

♥ = Part of population of singles in New York City wanting to marry

AGE GROUP	TOTAL OF SINGLE WOMEN	SINGLE MEN	THOSE WANTING TO MARRY SINGLE WOMEN	SINGLE MEN
21–34	235,986	186,658	27,986	156,987
35–44	167,890	156	127,890	2*
45–54	134,879	234	134,879	.05**

* These two men are Sam Debittle from Queens and Marty Cain from Brooklyn.

** Guy Trombone, a fifty-three-year-old bachelor from Valley Stream, claims he might be available if he could only find a "gal who's really loaded and who cooks as good as my mommy."

When asked about the problems of their social life, most of the women sounded confused and bitter.

"What can I say? It's the pits," claimed Tiffany Detroit, a thirty-four-year-old kindergarten teacher from Brooklyn. "I never meet any guys over five years old."

"At least they're single," countered a twenty-nine-year-old hairdresser who asked to remain anonymous. "You sound like you're in a great location to meet unmarried guys. The only men I meet on the job are the ones with better makeup than me."

Women at this meeting acknowledged that the holidays and the weekends were the hardest times for them. Several women reported working on Sundays in order to avoid seeing all the couples and families having brunch or walking on the street.

"I like to spend time pampering myself on the weekends," claimed another single woman who also asked that her name be withheld. "I get into a hot bathtub on Friday night and I don't get out again until I have to go to work on Monday morning."

"Aren't you as wrinkled as an old prune by then, Betty Martin?" this reporter inquired.

"You bitch!" Betty screamed. "I told you not to mention my name!"

With a few exceptions, most of the women at the bar expressed regret that they would probably not have children of their own. "I'll never be able to manipulate a child the way Mom manipulated me," sighed one lady who'd consumed fifteen banana daiquiris and was laid out on top of the bar. "That's why I drink," she explained before passing out.

This reporter left the Dew Drop Inn with a greater understanding of the plight of the single woman and a bar tab like you wouldn't believe.

But these observations are not a reason for single women to despair; they are the reason for them to persevere.

From Adam's first "date" with Eve to the courtship of Ben and J-Lo and then the *Alias* girl, dating has always been a test of personal endurance. And it always will be because, as the sign above the bar at the Dew Drop Inn read: "If God meant life to be easy for singles, why did He create New Year's Eve?"

dating for fun and profit

a financial overview

Dating is probably the most important aspect of a single person's life. A huge amount of time, effort, and money is invested in dating, yet very little planning is applied to this crucial area.

In our professional lives, we spend an extraordinary amount of energy developing plans to achieve our projected goals. We are a generation who worships at the MBA shrine. We believe in cost projections and profit-and-loss statements. So, why haven't we applied these basic techniques to our social lives?

When was the last time you sat down and charted a business plan for your dating career? When was the last time you tabulated your cost-per-unit date? When was the last time you inventoried your backlist of social engagements? If your answer is, "I don't have the foggiest idea what that means," then this chapter is for you.

Here is where you'll learn to chart your social life, to prepare a business plan for your dating career, and to analyze a potential date's assets and debits. You'll establish a profit center for your social life and learn how to depreciate your last boyfriend as easily as your car.

This may be the most important chapter you'll ever read, so pay attention. If you need to go the bathroom, then do it now.

dating business plan

THE MARKETPLACE

According to *Dating Industry Trends*, a professional magazine covering the singles market, up until the late 1980s dating was a routine activity involving fast cars, punk rock, cheap wine, and big hair. Today, dating is more complicated.

Kirby Denver, editor of *Dating Trends*, says, "We describe dating in the 2000s as being like the classic Roller Derby, a life-threatening contest to determine who will get dumped first."

While socializing is more extensive today than ever before, dating is experiencing a downward spiral in some respects. *Dating Trends* has predicted that from 2004 to 2010, the incidence of dating will increase 10 percent in units and 47 percent in dollars, while decreasing 97 percent in personal satisfaction. The increased population will account for the rise in units, inflation will account for the rise in dollars, and bad press about various social diseases will account for the decrease in satisfaction.

Who is affected by this trend? The market for dating has traditionally been generalized as the "under thirty-five" age group. This is due to several factors. Historically, people over thirty-five have been thought to be too smart to still be dating. Prior dating experience in high school, college, and in the workplace was considered enough to encourage most people to marry the first person who'd consent to have them.

Because of this, most rational thinkers projected the demise of dating. Yet, for the past three decades, dating has continued despite the fact that birth control pills cause cancer, herpes is incurable, and there's not a single humorous remark anyone can make about AIDS. Still, dating continues to prosper. This leads most experts to conclude:

1. People are either incredibly stupid or unbelievably horny.
2. The staying power of dating is beyond the scope of rational thinking. According to Dr. Donald Rumbacon, a physicist with the Arkansas Atomic Energy Commission, "We have projected that the only things to survive a nuclear holocaust will be the household cockroach and the blind date."

FREQUENCY

Every weekday in this country, there are approximately 37,895,987 dates. Of this figure, approximately 22,456,789 are complete bummers. While this leaves 15,439,198 so-called successful dates, none of them happen to me or the people I hang with.

During any given week, these numbers remain relatively constant from Tuesday to Friday. The number of dates drops radically, however, on Saturday, when most married men return home to their wives.

DATING SPREADSHEET

breakdown by type of date

	jan.	feb.	march	april	
blind dates					
first dates					
married men dated					
younger men dated					
dating disasters					
pickups/one-night stands					
affairs (more than 1 date)					
relationships (more than 2 dates)					
TOTAL DATES PER MONTH					

Conversely, the number of blind dates and first dates increases on Saturday night as single women attempt to make their married boyfriends jealous.

Sunday-night dates, while numerous, appear to end early, usually before dark, because, no matter how old or sophisticated a person gets, they always think of Sunday as a "school night."

According to the latest government census, on Monday nights everyone stays home to study the latest issue of *People* magazine.

may	june	july	aug.	sept.	oct.	nov.	dec.

INVENTORY AND BACKLIST

The strength of any business rests in its backlist and inventory, and the same is true for your social life. Dr. Marcia Quisont, a PhD in manic datology (the study of dating patterns among depressed singles) at Columbia University, has developed a backlist spreadsheet that the layperson can use to inventory her social warehouse.

COMMENTS

1. In terms of units, this spreadsheet can help you determine your most heavily dated months. Think about why you were so popular during that particular time frame. Were you wearing anything new? Did you have a new haircut? Were you frequenting a new singles bar? Doing drugs?

2. If the number zero (0) crops up more than thirty-nine times in this chart, you need to increase your monthly unit dates. You are obviously not getting out enough.

3. If you are heavy in the pickups/one-night stands column but weak in first dates, then you may want to reassess your criteria for selecting a guy to escort you home.

4. If you are heavy in the blind dates column but weak on affairs or relationships, you need a better set of friends fixing you up.

5. If your only completed category is dating disasters, you need Dr. Phil's books, tapes, and daily shots of his profound television wisdom. You need to get real, girlfriend!

ADVERTISING AND PROMOTION

One way to increase your number of unit dates is to concentrate on marketing and selling your product (namely, yourself). You may need to invest in advertising space to promote yourself to the general male public. You should not be embarrassed or dismiss this idea out of hand. One of the major themes of dating in the 2000s is clear to anyone who owns a laptop: it pays to pop up.

On almost every Web site from *Yahoo!* to *Stench: The Website of the Dead Fish Industry*, singles ads are the largest growing area of advertising revenue. Pretty soon these sites will be 90 percent singles ads and only 10 percent feature stories and ads for lower mortgage rates.

Unfortunately, this glut of electronic matchmaking greatly decreases your chance of meeting anyone. With so much competition in the field, you need to be more original.

Use your imagination. For instance, the perfect place to advertise is your car. Get in on the "Baby on Board" placard fad. Use your back window to declare "Single on Board" or "Dateless on Board."

Paint your cell phone number on the back window. Or get your phone number on a vanity license plate: 555-5555.

Post bumper stickers that declare: I BRAKE FOR SINGLE MEN; I BRAKE FOR CUTE GUYS; I'D RATHER BE ON A DATE; I BLIND DATE, DO YOU?; HONK IF YOU'RE FREE FOR DINNER!

If you don't own a car, use any of these clever slogans in your own original way—on a T-shirt or baseball hat, or tattooed on your forehead. Design a hat with a light that blinks on when you are available for a date (a tactic that works for cabbies, why not you?). Wear a sandwich board or, if you live in a high-rent district, a croissant board.

If you can afford it, rent a billboard. Hire a skywriter. If it pays to advertise, remember it pays even more to advertise big!

PROFIT AND LOSS

Advertising dollars are only one of the factors you will need to consider when calculating your dating revenue. Naturally, a profitable social life begins with a reliable budget. To project a budget for the coming year, you need to tabulate your cost-per-unit date.

Your cost-per-unit date will vary according to such factors as the cost of your hair-care products, whether or not you went for that collagen mask during this month's facial, and if you ever again wear that red lace thong you purchased at Victoria's Secret during a wave of optimism. Using the following flow-chart, you can tally the total amount invested on any particular date. Calculating your dating debits will help you decide if the money spent was worth the investment. According to a reliable yuppie, "Your cost-per-unit date is your most reliable guideline in determining whether or not it pays to continue dating that certain guy."

COST-PER-UNIT DATE FLOWCHART

DOLLAR AMOUNT	TOM	DICK	HARRY
SELF			
clothes (include undergarments)			
hair			
shoes			
makeup (other cosmetics)			
bleach (hair, mustache, etc.)			
dry-cleaning bills			
manicure/pedicure			
fashion accessories			
HAIR			
cut			
equipment (dryer, flat iron, etc.)			
products (mousse, gels, sprays, etc.)			
utensils (barrettes, bows, etc.)			
APARTMENT/HOUSE			
food and drink			
maid fee			
laundry (sheets, towels, etc.)			

ENTERTAINMENT			
tickets (movie, concert, etc.)			
restaurant bill			
bar tab			
SUPPLIES			
ajax (for bathroom)			
contraceptive jelly/condoms (per gross)			
RESEARCH AND DEVELOPMENT:			
internet fees			
dating coach			
TRANSPORTATION			
car ($0.14 per mile)			
gas and tolls			
subway fare			
MISCELLANEOUS			
phone bill			
marital aids			
valium or other drugs			
diet food (previous to date)			
TOTAL DOLLAR AMOUNTS			

FORMULA

Once you have assessed the amount you spent on each particular date, you can easily calculate your cost-per-unit date. The formula is simple:

$$\frac{total\ dollar\ amount}{number\ of\ dates} = cost\text{-}per\text{-}unit\ date$$

For example, if you spent a total of $450 on Tom and dated him five times, figure:

$$\frac{\$450}{5} = \$90\ per\text{-}unit\ date$$

If, on the other hand, you spent $450 on Dick but dated him only twice, your unit cost would be much higher:

$$\frac{\$450}{2} = \$225\ per\text{-}unit\ date$$

Now, ask yourself, given the cost of Donna Karan in today's marketplace, was Dick worth $135 more *per date* than Tom?

COMMENTS

1. When calculating cost-per-unit date, take into account that none of these expenditures are tax deductible, although they really should be. This means that the money costs you even more than you think, a concept I never fully grasped but one that seems to enrage most accountants.
2. While the cost-per-unit date is an essential tool in today's dating market, it is not the only guideline to use. A very high cost-per-unit date can be mitigated by two factors:
   - Expensive gifts. For instance, in the above example, if Dick bought you an expensive gold watch for your birthday, you can throw these calculations out the window, along with Tom.
   - Great sex. If he's good in bed, he's worth every dime he costs you, and then some.

RESEARCH AND DEVELOPMENT

R&D is money you invest (often called venture capital) when your social life needs a complete overhaul. This can include a week at the Golden Door Spa in California or a session with a new therapist or dating coach (see page 45.) Venture capital is used to discover if there's a new and datable person underneath your current personality.

RETURN POLICY

All dates are returnable, no matter what he tells you.

SUBSIDIARY RIGHTS

Any income derived from selling material based on your date is the sole property of the person making the sale.

conclusions

STRENGTHS

a. Your social life is repairable.
b. You have good genes and clean underwear.
c. You are basically a nice person.
d. Your cat likes you.

WEAKNESSES

a. Your social life is costing too much money.
b. You need to date more.
c. Your gums bleed.

GOALS

a. Increase the number of dates.
b. Decrease your cost-per-unit date.
c. Get married, have a baby, live happily ever after.

preparing to

date

I only like two kinds of men:
domestic and imported.

MAE WEST

I often wish I had time to
cultivate modesty. . . . But I am
too busy thinking about myself.

EDITH SITWELL,
THE OBSERVER,
1950

how desperate are you?

Being dateless for an extended period of time can seriously (perhaps permanently) warp your perspective. You may experience a considerable drop in your expectations. You may pass from merely "hoping to meet the right man" into the dreaded psychotic state known to therapists as Dateless and Desperate (D&D).

Shrinks use the following question to test a patient's tendency to become hopelessly D&D. Read the story below carefully, putting yourself in this situation. Be sure to answer as openly and honestly as possible.

dateless and desperate (D&D) TEST

You meet a handsome man in the vegetable department of your local grocery. He asks for your help in selecting a ripe cantaloupe. You notice he is not wearing a wedding ring.

While you squeeze or sniff the fruit (depending on the method your mother taught you), you ask if he's new to the neighborhood.

"Not exactly," he replies. "I've sort of been out of town for the last few years."

"On business?" you ask, noticing his finely developed shoulders.

"Yeah, sort of," he sheepishly replies. "I've been in prison."

"Prison? Like, in jail?"

"Yeah," he says. "I murdered my wife, sort of."

WHAT IS YOUR IMMEDIATE RESPONSE?

a. You drop the melon, scream for help, and run like hell.
b. You hand the melon to the ex-con and quietly slink away from him.
c. You blink once and say, "Oh? Does that mean you're single?"

SCORE

If you answered (a), you are obviously desperate for attention. No one screams in the produce department without causing general havoc to the more delicate fruits. You need sexual satisfaction to calm your nerves. You are in the gravest danger of becoming a victim of the dreaded D&D syndrome.

A classic example of D&D, often cited by psychiatrists, is the case of poor Daisy Singer, a young woman who, in high school, was voted Most Likely to Live in New Jersey. Daisy's condition went generally unnoticed and untreated until the day she filled out a job application for a position as an assistant executive secretary for a major corporation.

When asked, *Are you married?*, Daisy wrote: "*No, but I'm not without a companion. For the past six years I've been dating my television or, as I like to tease myself, Romancing the Sony (ha-ha!).*

"*I see Sony almost every night. We share the laughter, the reality, the friends, the news, the embarrassment of poor bladder control. In short, Sony lights up my life.*

"*Oh, I've had lots of boyfriends, but none were as loyal as Sony—or as easy to satisfy. To turn on my Sony, all I have to do is press a button, which is sure a lot easier than wearing spike heels and a leather garter belt to bed.*"

The company psychiatrist who reviewed Daisy's application asked her to explain her lengthy response.

"Gee," Daisy replied, "I thought it was an essay question."

Fortunately, Daisy found help. She's been in treatment for the past five years and can now almost get through an entire date without humming a commercial jingle every few minutes.

Daisy's inspiring tale should serve to remind all of us that early detection is our best defense in the war against D&D.

women who
self-help too much

It is a well-established fact that women prone to becoming Dateless and Desperate (D&D) are generally intelligent and well read. Interested in improving their lot in life, these women work extremely hard to keep up with the current body of work in the self-help field. The problem is that the anxiety and fear of becoming D&D is often so great that these women become self-help-aholics. Known as a disease of denial, the self-help-aholic is totally obsessed with books of pop psychology.

The disease starts slowly with one self-help book per month, then escalates to two per month, then three, four, five, and so on. Before too long, these women cannot leave the house without a paperback book clutched in each hand.

The disease is difficult to cure because so much reading distorts the addict's sense of perception about the world and gives her the feeling that any problem can be solved as long as it's listed in the index.

The self-help-aholic quickly becomes the self-help-hypochondriac, absorbing into her personality every symptom detailed on the back covers of these books. This is when she is in serious danger of overimproving herself.

The chart on page 42 is a sampling of some of the symptoms of this insidious addiction. To test your own susceptibility to the disease, carefully review the listing of psychological conditions and check off any that you feel apply to you.

WILLIAM FOX

PRESENTS

ALPHA

THEDA BARA

-IN-

UNDER THE YOKE

THE BATTLE FOR LOVE OF A WOMAN WITH NO REGRETS

STORY BY GEORGE SCARBOROUGH   SCENARIO BY ADRIAN JOHNSON

STAGED BY J·GORDON EDWARDS

A THEDA BARA SUPER PRODUCTION

FOX FILM CORPORATION

INSTANT SELF-ANALYSIS MENU

column A	column B
a woman with seven habits	a woman with the power of positive thinking
a woman who loves too much	a woman who found the cheese
a woman addicted to unhappiness	a woman who wins friends and influences people
a woman whose self matters	a woman with a chicken soup soul
a woman with 101 power thoughts	a woman who doesn't sweat the small stuff

SCORE

select	to get diagnosed
one from column A or B	mildly paranoid
one from A and one from B	lacking self-esteem
two from A and one from B	medium paranoid
two from A and two from B	without any esteem
three from A and two from B	paranoid and depressed
four from A and three from B	comes with egg roll
all of the above	a woman who reads too much

If you understand even part of this chart, clearly you have spent too much time reading self-help books and thinking about what's wrong with you. Your mind has been hopelessly warped by *Dr. Phil*, *For Love or Money*, and those four cranky women on *The View*. You are over-self-helped.

Granted, it is very difficult to be single in a self-help world. You are easy prey to the psychobabble of the so-called experts who write books about women's problems. You're confused and you want an easy answer. You're upset because none of these books have actually changed your life. You're distraught because you don't have a date for your cousin Debbie's wedding.

Quite simply, you are suffering from what psychologist Dr. Daniel Killjoy calls The Toto Dilemma.

As explained by Dr. Killjoy: "The Toto Dilemma is when women allow men, particularly handsome male authors like myself, to treat them like dogs. You put a good-looking guy like me on *Oprah* and all I have to do is say, 'Fetch,' and women flock to the bookstores for my book. Women today are in serious danger of turning self-help into self-destruct. That's why I wrote my book—to cash in on this situation."

Unlike most of the popular self-help books cited in the Instant Self-Analysis Menu, Dr. Killjoy's recently published book, *The Toto Dilemma: When Authors Treat You Like Dogs!*, does not claim to have the answer for achieving inner peace. In fact, Dr. Killjoy seriously doubts the existence of such a phenomenon. In his opening paragraph, he quotes the philosopher and fashion sage Fran Lebowitz, who said, "There is no such thing as inner peace. There's only nervousness and death."

Dr. Killjoy's thesis also differs radically from other popular self-help books in that he does not put a lot of emphasis on self-esteem. "Self-esteem has become the iPod of the pop psychology field; everyone's got to have it. I wonder why?" he asks in the first chapter, entitled "I'd Divorce Myself, If I Could." "There are only three things you basically need to improve your life: (1) a good hair colorist; (2) a guest bathroom; and (3) at least one vibrating appliance."

To this end, Dr. Killjoy recommends that you immediately stop reading other people's self-help books and concentrate solely on his book. "We're not in Kansas anymore," says the doctor. "We must prepare ourselves to enter the dating market."

The Toto Dilemma is loaded with down-to-earth advice for successful dating. For example, Dr. Killjoy recommends that you avoid materialistic considerations and be more realistic when dating a man for the first time. "Remember it's not how much money your date spends on you that counts," writes Dr. Killjoy. "What really matters is what kind of car he drives."

His advice is to avoid jeopardizing your first date by living in the future and to try not to be concerned with security. As Dr. Killjoy points out: "You can never fully own another human being, although sometimes you can rent with an option to buy."

The Toto Dilemma shows you how to get out of your self-imposed doghouse by teaching you the following:

- Where your extra erogenous zones are located and whether you have to pay a toll to get to them.

- Why, when you are good, you are very, very good, but when you are bad, you date more.

- How to lie down and roll over, along with 167 other ways to say "I love you."

- Why your two most compatible astrology signs are Slim and None.

"Do not go gentle into Saturday night," advises Dr. Killjoy. "With *The Toto Dilemma,* you can join the mass of women leading lives of noisy desperation."

hiring a dating coach

As if there aren't enough schools of therapy available today, many professionals are now opening practices that specialize in the problems of the dateless. For $140 an hour, you can have a session with someone who can, presumably, direct you down the road to romance.

Beverly Grossman, a thirty-nine-year-old social worker from Saint Paul, Minnesota, recently opened a Dating Clinic and Laundromat in the Twin Cities called Studs and Suds. "I prefer to start sessions during presoak and finish by the first rinse cycle," says Grossman, a pretty brunette with a flair for capes and cowboys boots. "But sometimes they last well into the spin cycles."

Grossman treats only people (most of her clients are woman, of course) who are serious about meeting a mate, and each client must commit to a seven-month treatment program. (They are allowed to quit early only if they meet someone who Grossman deems appropriate.) Clients are required to spend one hour a week with Grossman (where they are encouraged to bring along their dirty laundry), spend at least twenty-two hours on the "lookout," and go on at least one date. "Dating is like using the treadmill," says Grossman in defense of her strenuous program. "If you don't do it often enough, you might as well not do it at all."

The purpose of the sessions is to break old habits, dissect dates, and formulate strategies to energize a client's social life. "I tell the nymphos to cut it out and the prudes to spice it up. I advise the stagnators to quit stalling and the aggressors to ease on down the road. You'd think the job would be pretty hard but it's amazingly simple. Don't tell anyone I said this, but any idiot could be a dating coach."

Grossman is a strong advocate of Internet dating and for

an additional fee, she will edit and polish all e-mail corre-spondence for her clients. "This is a very time-consuming courtesy that I extend only to my favored clients," the coach notes, "but since I charge by the hour, I really don't mind doing it."

Like any therapist, Grossman is on call for her most severe cases. Her cell phone rings constantly as clients call to relate the intimate details of every encounter with their perspective dates. "It's like having a best friend," says Nancy Miller, a longtime client of Studs and Suds, "except better because, when I talk to Bev, it's all about me."

learning to compromise
a personal note

Before we delve into the specifics of getting and keeping a date, I wanted to interject a personal note about the fine art of compromising.

Now, this comes from a woman who was raised to believe that I'd never have to settle for less than my ideal.

My mother always told me that there were plenty of fish in the sea and that somewhere out there was the man of my dreams.

Of course, one must take into account the fundamental difference between dating in Mom's day and in mine. In my mother's time, it was a shock to hear a man say, "Frankly, my dear, I don't give a damn." Today, it's a surprise when a date doesn't say it.

Still, I had my standards and, of course, I was young enough to believe my mother knew what she was talking about when she said, "There's a lid for every pot."

Consequently, over the years, I developed and refined a long list of everything I wanted in a mate. Here's what my perfect "lid" would be like: He should be tall, dark, and handsome (of course); rich, famous, and successful; thoughtful, romantic, sensitive, gentle, and good-natured. He should excel at sports and be kind to animals, relatives, and me. He had to love kids, my funny smile, and walks by the beach. He should be a good dancer, if not a great one, and it was essential that he know how to dress. No part of his person should smell bad.

It was a definite negative if he was fond of contact sports, but, in all fairness, I supposed that I could learn to adapt to the occasional football game on Sunday afternoon, as long as it didn't interfere with our weekend visits to my mom.

From this list, you might not be surprised to learn that I never married.

Well, times have changed.

I've gotten older. Much older. I eventually had to acknowledge that maybe I was being a little too choosy. After several years, and $26,000 in therapy, I am now more realistic.

I've refined my requirements somewhat. Now I'm looking for a man who holds down a steady job and isn't carrying an infectious disease.

And, frankly, if he has trouble making a living, well, I can accept that. I suppose, with my successful career, I could support both of us; but I'm real firm on the disease part—at least I think I am.

Actually, I exaggerate. I haven't abandoned *all* my standards. I do have two absolute requirements. I will not go out with a man who wears more jewelry than me, and I'll never, ever go to bed with a guy who calls me Babe. Other than that, however, I'm real flexible.

When Oprah Winfrey was once asked about love by *People* magazine, she replied, "My idea of heaven is a great big baked potato and someone to share it with." Notice that she put the baked potato first. No wonder we love Oprah.

One of the more fundamental truths about dating is that you can learn more from Sophie Tucker than from your own mother. Sophie once said: "From birth to age eighteen, a girl needs good parents, from eighteen to thirty-five she needs good looks, from thirty-five to fifty-five she needs a good personality, and from fifty-five on she needs cash."

Sophie Tucker was one really together lady. I wish I knew the name of her therapist.

25 snappy comebacks to

"why aren't you married yet?"

1. "You haven't asked yet."
2. "Johnny Depp is taken."
3. "What? And spoil my great sex life?"
4. "I look awful in white."
5. "Because I love hearing this question."
6. "Just lucky, I guess."
7. "It gives my mother something to live for."
8. "My fiancé is awaiting his parole."
9. "I'm still hoping for a shot at Miss America."
10. "Do you know how hard it is to get *two* tickets to *Wicked*?"
11. "I'm waiting until I get to be your age."
12. "It didn't seem worth a blood test."
13. "I already have enough laundry to do, thank you."
14. "Because I think it would take all the spontaneity out of dating."
15. "My co-op board doesn't allow husbands."
16. "I'd have to forfeit my billion-dollar trust fund."
17. "They just opened a great singles bar on my block."
18. "I wouldn't want my parents to drop dead from sheer happiness."
19. "I guess it just goes to prove that you can't trust those voodoo-doll rituals."
20. "What? And lose my lifetime membership in eHarmony?"
21. "We really want to, but my boyfriend's wife just won't go for it."
22. "I don't want to have to support another person on my paycheck."
23. "Why aren't you thin?"
24. "I'm married to my career, although recently, we have been considering a trial separation."
25. *Bonus reply for single mothers:* "Because having a husband and a child would be redundant."

how to get a
date

She who hesitates is not only lost
but miles from the next exit.

UNKNOWN

A fresh start is an illusion,
but a necessary one.

HELEN ROWLAND,
A GUIDE TO MEN,
1922

places to
meet men

You do not need to be a dating genius to know you cannot start dating without first meeting. Meeting is, in fact, the crucial first step in the dating process.

In olden times, men and women had it easy. When they were ready to start dating, their parents contacted the local matchmaker, who selected an appropriate candidate and arranged for the first date. (This worked well because no one had voice mail in those days.)

The purpose of these arranged meetings was marriage, and, with a big enough dowry, most women could count on getting married or, at the very least, asked out a second time. Not a bad arrangement, if you ask me.

Matchmaking has been much maligned in this century, mainly due to mediocre revivals of *Fiddler on the Roof*, and is all but lost to us as a viable option for single people. This is unfortunate, especially for women with trust funds, who were traditionally favored by matchmakers. However, as my Nana Sunshine would say, there's no use crying over spilt milk. Those days are long gone, and now we're left to our own devices.

Let's face it, it's not easy to meet men because it's not easy to *find* them.

The key is knowing where to look.

bars

Of course, the most obvious place is your neighborhood bar. You don't need to watch beer commercials to know how much men like to drink. But you can substantially increase your odds of meeting a man by knowing the best time to hit the bars. You can find this out by checking your local newspaper for listings of major sports events. If you don't know all that much about sports (and what single woman really does? Or cares?), be advised to look for events that include the following words: *Play-off*, *Series*, or *Bowl*. Pay particular attention when these words are aggrandized, as in *World* Series or *Super* Bowl. The more adjectives they add to these events, the better.

Remember, during this time, to frequent only bars with television sets. In fact, you can pretty much ratio the size of the TV screen to the number of men in attendance (i.e., the bigger the screen, the bigger the crowd). Hit Madison Square Garden during one of those closed-circuit boxing events and you might fill your social calendar for a month.

Arrive at your selected establishment several hours before the event takes place so that you're assured a well-positioned bar stool. That way, if you don't meet anyone special, you can sell your seat when you leave.

co-op meetings

If you're interested in meeting a man who owns real estate (and who isn't?), then you'd be wise to attend as many co-op meetings as possible but never in your own building. You don't ever want to date one of your neighbors, because you'll never again be able to do your laundry in the basement without first putting on makeup and deodorant. Who needs that kind of aggravation? No, you should only attend co-op meetings in buildings other than your own. Ask your friends to invite you to their annual meetings (and remember to reciprocate the favor).

If your friends tell you their meetings are "closed to the public," they may be keeping these social events to themselves, so you'll need to be more inventive and find new friends. You can find out when a particular building is holding a shareholders' meeting by scanning the bulletin boards in apartment house lobbies or by bribing the doormen. (Check with your accountant as such "tips" are probably tax-deductible expenses.)

If you don't own a co-op, you should try even harder to meet a man who does. As your mother would say, it's just as easy to fall in love with a man who owns real estate as it is to fall in love with one who rents.

reunions

I discovered that high school reunions are excellent places to meet men. In general, people attend their reunions only if they've achieved a relative measure of success in life and if they're looking for a date. But, be forewarned, the same rule applies here as in co-op meetings. Go to anyone else's reunion but your own. At your own high school reunion you'll only be reminded of what the man shortage means to you—namely, that guys you wouldn't let near your locker in high school are now snubbing you. This is not a lesson you need to learn more than once.

I'll share with you another depressing lesson that might come your way if you are foolish enough to attend your own high school reunion. I made that mistake and thought I had a pretty good time until I discussed the event with Dr. Yesandno, my shrink at the time. Now, admittedly, I was pretty full of myself during that session, bragging about how I was obviously one of the most successful of all my past classmates. "Most of them work *locally*," I scoffed, "they never even made it out of New Jersey!"

The doctor shrugged. "Well, maybe they were happy there and didn't feel the need to escape."

Happy? In high school? In New Jersey? The thought had never ever entered my consciousness and, in fact, depressed me so much that I upped my sessions to three times a week for the next several years.

off-track betting (OTB)

If you're not too choosy, you might want to check out OTB or make a quick tour of your local racetrack. Betting establishments attract men like flies to honey, and, as I said, if you're not particular about dating certain species of insects, OTB may be the place for you.

Other gambling establishments, casinos, for example, are also excellent sources of male companionship. At a blackjack table in Puerto Rico, I once met a young rabbinical student who I subsequently dated for six months back home in New York City. I know that sounds like a joke but it is 100 percent true. He was a nice guy, too, though I had to stop seeing him after he confessed that he could not break his habit of visiting massage parlors in Times Square. I often wonder if he ever continued with his rabbinical studies.

the pipeline

If you are willing to travel, or just superdesperate, the best place in the world to meet unattached men is on the Alaska pipeline. I'm told that the trek through the frozen tundra is well worth the effort for any woman who wants to know what it feels like to be Angelina Jolie.

police stations and firehouses

Getting arrested is a great way to meet a good-looking cop. Remember, too, that policemen, like firemen, are accustomed to making house calls. A minor fire or an imagined robbery can fill your living room with handsome men in uniform.

I nearly swooned when my next-door neighbor set fire to her kitchen and a dozen gorgeous guys carried all this heavy equipment up eleven flights in our building. Oh my, they were so sweaty and red faced and so young and handsome—even through the clouds of smoke in the hallways. The firemen wanted me to vacate the building, but I insisted on hanging around just in case any of them needed mouth-to-mouth.

emergency rooms

Overdose, very carefully, after making arrangements for a good friend to come calling no more than seven seconds after you ingest your drug of choice. In the ambulance, or at the hospital, give your card to all doctors, residents, male nurses, or other personnel who look like potential dating material.

cyberspace

Of course, no serious discussion of dating in the 2000s would be complete without a few words about Internet Dating, an inevitable way station on the information superhighway. We live in a society that turns to the computer to outsource everything, so why not try outsourcing your social life?

For anyone who has been living in a cave for the past five years, Internet Dating is a process whereby you connect to an online dating service, write the most ridiculous lies about yourself, post a photo from ten years and twenty pounds ago, and then wait to hear back from someone who has concocted his own Photoshopped version of himself and his life.

The crazy thing is, it sometimes works.

I have a cousin who met his current wife online, and I know two other couples who are now dating and may eventually marry after connecting in cyberspace. Still I find the entire procedure nothing short of bizarre. What happened to the romance of spotting a pair of dark blue eyes across a crowded room? What's romantic about getting an e-mail from a complete stranger? Don't we have enough strangers e-mailing us with great deals for new mortgage rates, prescription drugs, porno sites, and teeth whiteners?

Of course, like everyone else, I tried Internet Dating a couple of times. I was not as successful as my cousin. I met one guy for brunch and neither of us could get out of the restaurant fast enough. I met a second guy for a drink and really kind of liked him. He said he would call me. That was thirteen months ago and I am still waiting. I am giving him six more months, tops, and then, forget it, it is over between us. I mean it. Okay, maybe seven months, but then I am really breaking up with him.

speedy dating

Like speed-reading, Speedy Dating was invented to increase quantity and decrease quality in your life. It is a process whereby you have not one, but thirty or forty little dates in a single evening. You can choose from various companies offering parties that last for three hours with up to thirty-five three-minute dates or, for those who prefer more depth to their social life, two-hour parties of ten-minute dates with eight to ten people. Speedy Dating is a lot like the orgy scene of the 1970s, without the sex of course.

Speedy Dating was invented and trademarked by an international Amish educational network but has been ripped off by companies of many other lifestyles and renamed Quicky Dates, Munchkin Dates, Three-Minute Dates, Four-Minute Dates, Four-Minute Thirty-Second Dates, Five-Minute Dates, and, oh well, you get the idea.

The advantages of Speedy Dating are that you are guaranteed more dates in one evening than you will probably enjoy in an entire year. And you can do it all in one pair of panty hose. Also, you avoid the embarrassment of sitting through a whole lobster dinner with someone you wouldn't want to introduce to your dog trainer.

It works like this: you enter a restaurant and each table is assigned a number. A potential date is sitting at each table. Someone rings a bell and, hooray!, the Speedy Dating begins. You sit yourself down at the table, talk for a few minutes, a bell rings, and you move on to the next table and your next minuscule date.

At the start of the evening you are given a scorecard and, after each Munchkin date, you check a box. You are either interested in the person at table 21 (check YES), or not (check NO), and so on, until you've marked all the empty boxes. At the end of the evening, the scorecards are turned in and tabulated and, a few days later, you are notified if any of your YES responses matched those of anyone else's. Your best bet, of course, is to check YES for every one of your minuscule dates, although the person who tallies your scorecard may not take you seriously if you do.

Some participants want to know what they should wear for their Munchkin dates. Well, if you ask me, you should dress appropriately in a business suit or dress and wear comfortable shoes, and a little lipstick wouldn't hurt either. Bathing suits, leather thongs, dog collars, gold lamé, and slinky nightgowns are generally frowned upon.

What should you discuss with your Munchkin date? You may talk about anything *except* sex, politics, religion, your mother, his mother, sports, family matters, food, pending lawsuits, music, health issues, archeology, what you wore to your prom, reality television, your phobias or perversions, films, work-related problems, your manicurist, the Middle East, your blood alcohol level, carpentry, past relationships, current relationships, the tsetse fly, your weight, what you wanted to be in third grade, Mel Gibson, what you did last summer, Britney Spears, outstanding traffic tickets, when you began (and/or stopped) menstruation, your current mortgage rate, yoga, the weather, how you like your coffee in the morning, prescription drugs, where you went to high school, your marital status, how many frequent-flyer miles you have, stretch marks, how you would redecorate the Speedy Dating room, allergies, your ATM password, O. J. Simpson, that blonde girl who lost her arm to a shark bite, your pets, Switzerland, where you bought your outfit, the Olympics, David Letterman, your name, your address, your social security number, or, finally, how much you paid for your car insurance. Other than that, the sky's the limit.

You may think that three minutes is not long enough to tell if you would want to date this person across the table, but you are wrong. As any woman bent on marriage will confirm, three minutes is plenty of time to determine how your minuscule date will look in a tux when he is walking down the aisle.

miscellaneous

Group therapy meetings and bankruptcy court are good places for finding desperate (i.e., vulnerable) men. If you sign up for jury duty, you can serve your civic duty and, even more important, find guys who are so bored out their minds that they'll be up for almost anything.

Other places to meet men include pool halls, construction sites, military installations, golf courses, Boy Scout meetings (if you're into the younger-man thing), porno movie houses, sperm banks, steam rooms, prisons, ballparks, and the men's department of Bloomingdale's, if you have the energy.

There is an alternative to going out and finding a man—which brings us to the horrific blind date.

the woman who

mistook her blind date for a
potential husband

Everyone knows that the best policy is to not expect miracles from life. "I didn't want to be rich," Kate (Mrs. Zero) Mostel once claimed, "I just wanted enough to get the couch reupholstered."

Still, when you go out on a blind date, it's hard not to entertain the following fantasy:

The doorbell rings. You get up from your dressing table, take one last lingering look at yourself in the mirror, and nod with approval. You open the front door.

He stands in the doorway, but you can barely see his face behind all of those enormous yellow roses he's holding in his hands. He presents you with the bouquet.

He is incredibly tall and looks like a cross between George Clooney, Jon Stewart, and the guy you loved madly in sixth grade.

His crooked smile reveals his vulnerability, a great set of real white teeth, and a neat dimple in his left cheek.

He is rendered speechless by your beauty and falls instantly in love with you.

The next day, you discover he is a millionaire brain surgeon/criminal lawyer/architect who pilots his own Lear jet, climbs mountains, volunteers time to care for sick children, loves to dance, and owns oceanfront property.

Say hello to your dream blind date. Say good-bye to reality.

The blind date is genuine proof that truth is stranger than fiction. The facts speak for themselves:

A perfect stranger calls you up. You have an extremely uncomfortable conversation, which you both pretend to enjoy. He asks you to see a movie that you have no interest in seeing. You worry about what to wear, what he'll look like, and whether you'll have anything to discuss with him.

In your heart of hearts, you know you will have a terrible time, the date will be a total washout. But, still, you have an anxiety attack if your hair frizzes while you are getting ready for him to arrive.

Your tendency during this initial stage of anxiety is to curse the friend or relative responsible for arranging the date. Try to avoid hating this person.

It is best to remember that the people who set you up on blind dates have the best of intentions, really they do. You need to keep this in mind, because the truth is you can never, never believe what anyone tells you when they describe the person you are being fixed up with.

If you're told, for instance, that your blind date looks like a movie star, you're not told that the movie star is Steve Buscemi.

If you're told that your blind date is a great catch, you're not told that his wife's alimony lawyer has been trying to catch him for months.

If you're told this is a match made in heaven, you're not told it was on an off day.

If you're told your blind date is an old-fashioned guy, you're not told that this applies mainly to his clothes.

But, hey! You're single, and although your phone rings constantly, it's always your mother calling.

It is a well-known fact, by the way, that the worst blind dates, bar none, are those arranged by your mother. It doesn't matter whether the guy is a district attorney, a genius, a bestselling writer, or an Olympic athlete. If your mother found him, he's a geek.

Regardless, you want to take advantage of every opportunity, so you accept blind date after blind date. Eventually, however, your inner psyche begins to rebel.

Your cousin Rhonda offers to fix you up with her brother's accountant, but instead you choose to stay home and watch *Survivor*.

Your best friend meets a great new guy and you forget to ask if he has any single friends.

You make a firm decision that blind dating is not for you. You begin to consider the alternatives: celibacy or surrogate dating.

an alternative to blind dates

surrogate dating

Until fairly recently (March 16, 1999, to be specific), single people didn't have much of an alternative to blind dating. A blind date was something you suffered through in order to tell yourself you were doing everything possible to enhance your social life. As we all know, everything changed with the advent of surrogate dating.

Surrogate dating, the practice of hiring a substitute person to date for you, was inadvertently invented by Mindy Wonger, a thirty-nine-year-old stenographer from Pasadena, California. Mindy, single and sorry, answered the phone one day and found herself accepting a blind date from Dave, an acquaintance of Mindy's Al-Anon qualifier.

After hanging up the phone, Mindy realized she'd rather walk barefoot on a bed of glass than go on another blind date, yet she was afraid to cancel the date with Dave. Except for her nightly Al-Anon meetings, Mindy hadn't gone out in three months, and, as every single woman knows, opportunity doesn't knock all that often after you've been diagnosed as a Woman Who Never Learned the Rules.

Mindy solved her problem by hiring her roommate, Carla, to date Dave. In exchange for not having to clean the bathroom for two weeks, Carla agreed to masquerade as Mindy and to have dinner with Dave. Carla wore a wig and Mindy's Dolce & Gabbana jumpsuit. Carla also promised not to fall in love and to return Dave to Mindy in the event he proved to be marriage material.

Thus, the first surrogate dating arrangement was made.

Today, surrogate dating is a bit more complex, since not everyone has a roommate who looks good in Dolce & Gabbana. Agencies such as The Next Best Thing in Atlanta have been established to match clients and surrogate dates. Prospective clients can select surrogates with the same hair color and body type. Just Like You in Jacksonville, Florida, organizes their employee surrogate pool into nine basic personality categories. Clients can decide for themselves which "type" best matches their personality and can choose from the following classifications: Princess, Workaholic, Hippie, Easily Addicted, Punk, Sex Symbol, Homebody, Artist, and Adaptable to Anything He Wants.

Fees up to $2,000 have been paid, especially when the date has been arranged through the parents of either of the parties involved. And, because money is now involved, written contracts are not uncommon.

Surrogate contracts specify such contingencies as additional bonus payments to rehire the surrogate for the couple's first fight or for their first "totally honest" discussion about previous sexual encounters, whichever comes first.

Surrogate dating has drastically reduced blind dating and, up until recently, was considered a boon for the singles market. In late 1999, Club Med established a Club Surrogate on St. Luigi's Island where guys and gals who were too shy to travel alone could hire a surrogate to vacation for them while they stayed home and watched television. *People* magazine interviewed five surrogate singles for their September 23, 1999, issue. In late fall of the same year, Candace Bushnell published a hip novel about the New York surrogate dating scene. And a January 2000 episode of *Friends* featured Ross on a surrogate date.

Then, suddenly, surrogate dating was nearly brought to a screeching halt by Mary Beth Whiteface and Elysse Sterp in their now legendary lawsuit, *Sterp v. Whiteface.*

The shocking case began in April of 2000, when Mary Beth Whiteface was hired by Elysse Sterp to date Marvin Slavin, a nephew of Ms. Sterp's mother's canasta partner. Mary Beth was promised full combat pay because the date involved not only Ms. Sterp's mother but her mother's canasta partner, who was also a second cousin and a bigmouth like you wouldn't believe.

Although Mary Beth claimed she only took the job out of pity for the dateless Elysse, lawyers for Ms. Sterp maintained it was no coincidence that in March of 2000, Mary Beth suffered a serious shopping attack in Bloomingdale's, specifically in the Ghost department, and desperately needed the cash.

Whatever her motives, and much to her surprise, Mary Beth enjoyed her date with Marvin. In fact, she had such a good time, she decided to keep Marvin all to herself.

In complete violation of her contract with Elysse, Mary Beth introduced Marvin to her parents.

In testimony to the court, Mary Beth later explained, "Your Honor, it was just one of those things, one of those crazy flings."

"A trip to the moon on gossamer wings?" prompted Ms. Whiteface's lawyer.

"Just one of those things," sighed Mary Beth, choking back her tears.

"One of those bells that now and then rings, I suppose," scoffed Elysse Sterp.

The most damaging argument the clever district attorney used against Mary Beth was the fact she'd neglected to tell Elysse that, on their first date, Mary Beth and Marvin engaged in a long walk by the ocean while Marvin recited his favorite lines from Woody Allen movies. (Beach walks are absolutely forbidden during surrogate dating. In fact, the rules of surrogate dating discourage encounters near any body of water, including lakes, streams, rivers, indoor pools, and Jacuzzis. Especially Jacuzzis.)

Almost as damning, Mary Beth and Marvin ran off for the weekend to the mountains. From Ye Olde Country Inn in Connecticut, Mary Beth called Elysse and pleaded to be released from her contract. When Elysse refused, Mary Beth threatened to tell Marvin that Elysse had once been a man named Elwyn.

After a long and arduous court battle, the judge decided in favor of Elysse Sterp, requiring Mary Beth Whiteface to honor her contractual obligation and to release Marvin Slavin from the Whiteface cellar. The judge further instructed Mary Beth to return Marvin's ID bracelet.

In Mary Beth's favor, the judge ruled that Marvin and Mary Beth could maintain non-weekend visitation rights, but only if they went Dutch treat.

The Whiteface/Sterp case has, of course, raised many complex questions about the moral and ethical basis for surrogate dating.

- Even though we have the technology to provide everyone with a surrogate date, do we have any moral obligation to be truthful with the people we date?

- Does Mary Beth Whiteface have the right to fall in love and abandon her contractual obligations?

- Did Elysse Sterp really have a sex-change operation?

The adverse publicity of the Whiteface/Sterp case has greatly decreased the practice of surrogate dating. Always controversial, surrogate dating is now even more opposed by conservatives, born-agains, krishnas, and most married people in general. The only groups still supporting surrogate dating are lawyers and a splinter group of radical feminists who feel women should have the legal right to do anything.

In spite of any opposition, however, surrogate dating is unlikely to go away. Anyone who has ever accepted a blind date because they needed to meet someone new knows that no price is too high to pay when contemplating the pain and agony of opening the front door on a complete stranger who, in all probability, has still not gotten over his last girlfriend.

how to call
a man for a date

Unfortunately, women like myself (broadly speaking, all females over the age of eighteen) are at a great disadvantage in today's dating marketplace. In our day (specifically the 1970s, 1980s, and even parts of the 1990s), only the guys had the privilege of choosing a prospective date and doing the asking. For girls, there was only one method for getting a date. You waited by your telephone for a guy to call. If he didn't call, you washed your hair.

Okay, so maybe it wasn't the most dynamic way to build a social life. In our defense, it was all we knew, never having been properly trained in the guerrilla dating tactics of today. (This is not our fault. Like most things that go wrong in our lives, we can blame our mothers for not adequately advising us.) Also, we didn't have Sarah Jessica Parker or Christina Aguilera as role models. Those of us who grew up with Ally McBeal, *Friends*, or Buffy may not have dated very much, but we had our dignity, our self-respect, our pride, and, for sure, we had clean hair.

Well, times have changed. Calling a guy for a date is as common today as Korean nail salons or Starbucks. Girls no longer stand on ceremony, and we older women need to adapt to these new ways. The 2000s demand aggression, guts, and lots of attitude. Women today must toss themselves into the dating pool, whether or not they wear a life preserver. Dating in the 2000s means: Sink or Swim or Get the Hell Out of the Pool!

The advantages of asking a man for a date are twofold. By making that call, you are taking control of your social life while at the same time gaining a unique opportunity to experience the heady power that comes from conquering your fear of rejection.

Calling a man for a date is a lot like learning how to insert a diaphragm; the first time is really embarrassing, but once you get used to the mess, you'll find the long-range advantages outweigh your initial repulsion.

If you are nervous about calling that cute guy you met in Kinko's, here are some useful suggestions to help build up your confidence.

You begin by convincing yourself to make that call. Stand in front of your bathroom mirror and tell yourself that you *will* call him. Persuade yourself that you actually *want* to call him, you *need* to call him. Concentrate on your image in the mirror. Remind yourself that this is not the face of a coward. Stare long and hard at yourself. (Warning: Do not get sidetracked into attacking any facial blemishes or bleaching some section of hair above your shoulders.)

If you are particularly nervous, it sometimes helps if you prepare for the worst-case scenario. A technique I often use when confronted with a difficult situation is to ask myself, What's the worst possible thing that could happen?

When I decided to call Darrell, a handsome man I'd taken home from a party one gloriously naughty evening, I asked myself this: What will happen if I call him?

I came up with the following list of possibilities:

a. He'll say yes.
b. He'll say no, but thank me for calling.
c. He'll say no, he can't go out with me because he forgot to mention he was attached to his wife, someone else's wife, a girlfriend, or a really weird pet.
d. He'll tell me to never call him again.

I prepared myself for each of the above contingencies. Whatever answer he gave, I was ready with a witty reply. I felt confident enough to make that phone call.

Just like a man, Darrell defied my list of possibilities, coming up with a scenario that was far beyond my imagination: Darrell didn't remember who I was. "I don't think I ever got your name," was the way Darrell explained his reaction.

My therapist artfully tried to comfort me. "At least you know the reason *why* Darrell hasn't called," Dr. Yesandno said, not unkindly.

"Yeah," I mumbled, "I suppose it's hard to call someone when you don't know their last name."

"Or their first name," my therapist, a real stickler for details, pointed out.

I waited six months before I called another male, other than Dr. Yesandno, of course.

I did, however, use the time productively by practicing my dialing skills. Every day I made at least two phony phone calls, pretending each time that I was calling Darrell. My therapist wondered why I wasn't arrested for public obscenity, even though I explained that most of the men I called seemed to actually enjoy my profanities.

Those phony phone calls taught me that practice was essential in order to "give good phone." Telephone technique is an acquired skill. By the time I was ready to call another man for a date, I had the confidence to forge ahead.

Since those early years, I have established a working routine that helps me overcome my shyness.

If you feel insecure about calling that special guy, try the following Nine-Step Program that I have developed. It works for me, maybe it'll work for you!

1. Drink a glass of wine, quickly.
2. Clutch a favorite teddy bear to your chest.
3. Practice what you are going to say by talking to your teddy bear.
4. Pick up the phone and place it in your lap. Take several deep breaths.
5. Carry phone and teddy bear to dining room table.
6. Crawl under table.
7. Grit teeth, hold breath, squeeze eyes shut, and pray.
8. Dial.
9. When a woman answers the phone, hang up.

While this routine works really well for me, there are several other methods that I have also tried, with varying degrees of success. If you are not comfortable calling him from your home, call him from a party or during another date. Make sure there is plenty of noise in the background. Pretend you are so busy this was the only free moment you had to call him.

Call him in the middle of the night. If you wake him from a deep sleep, you may catch him at a weak moment when he's likely to agree to just about anything.

Whichever method you choose, try not to panic during those excruciating moments after dialing but before the phone is answered, when "rrringg!" is the loneliest sound that you'll ever hear.

Keep an airsickness bag handy if you tend to panic under pressure and, for goodness sake, do not forget to self-medicate.

These moments will be among the longest and most stressful of your life. Your instinct will be to hang up, which you will probably do a few times before you are steady enough to allow him time to answer the phone.

The standard procedure, if you've called and then hung up, is to wait fifteen minutes before attempting to call again.

If, however, you've called, he's answered, and then you've hung up, the standard procedure is call back immediately and say that your phone is broken.

Between attempts to reach him, boost your own morale by reminding yourself how brave you are and what a good thing you are doing. You are back in the game, girlfriend! With a little bit of initiative, he will answer, say he's busy for the next six months, and you will be well on your way to your next major heartbreak.

Calling a man for a date is a real-life experience, one that all women should try at least once.

So, get out there with your cell phones and text message him for a date!

If you can't do it for yourself, then do it for the cause.

As women, we need to fight for the right to determine our dating destiny. What our feminist forepersons achieved for us in the boardrooms, we will now achieve in the bedroom.

As we move closer and closer to a nonsexist world, women will have an equal opportunity as men to be rejected, embarrassed, and humiliated.

CLARA **BOW**

in
AL. ROCKETT
PRODUCTION

HOOPL

with Presto

Richard CROMWELL   Herbert MUNDIN   James GLEAS

...LLOYD from the play "The Barker" by John Kenyon Nicholson stage play produced...

the first

date

I never liked the men I loved
and never loved the men I liked.

FANNY BRICE,
THE FABULOUS FANNY,
1952

Standing in the middle of the road
is very dangerous; you get knocked
down by traffic from both sides.

MARGARET THATCHER

I require only three things of a
man. He must be handsome,
ruthless, and stupid.

DOROTHY PARKER

getting ready for a date

in just under six hours

3:55 Go on diet to lose fifteen pounds in the next five hours.

4:00 Turn on *Dr. Phil.*

4:10 File nails.

4:20 Go to the kitchen and get a Diet Coke.

4:30 Polish nails.

4:35 Blow on nails.

4:36 Get impatient and wave hands in air. Knock over Diet Coke.

4:37 Curse.

4:38 Go to kitchen. Tear off paper towel carefully, using teeth.

4:45 Repolish nails on left hand. Try to be patient.

5:00 Run bath.

5:05 Call best friend and report how excited you are.

5:35 Answer doorbell. Be nice to irate downstairs neighbor. Tell him, "It's only water, for goodness sake!" Remind him that ceilings are replaceable, people are not.

5:36 Shut off running bathwater.

5:37 Get in tub.

5:38 Get out of tub to answer phone.

5:39 Scream at the person who dialed a wrong number.

5:40 Get back in tub.

5:41 Get out of tub to get another Diet Coke.

5:43 Get in tub.

5:44 Get out of tub to get apricot scrub cream.

5:45 Get in tub and fall asleep from exhaustion.

6:00 Dream about date. Remind yourself you only have three more hours left to get ready. Snap awake.

6:15 Wash hair, shave armpits and legs.

6:25 Towel-dry and comb hair.

6:30 Call second-best friend. Discuss what you should wear. Ask if you can borrow her new Prada dress. Hang up when she weasels out of the request with the lame excuse that she's wearing that dress tonight. Decide you need an alternative second-best friend.

6:45 Realize your hair is drying with funny ridges. Panic.

6:46 Run to bathroom.

6:46 Blow-dry hair.

6:50 Ditto.

7:00 Ditto.

7:01 Look in mirror. Want to puke. Curse parents' hair genes.

7:02 Plug in flat iron.

7:03 Inspect face in mirror. Decide *not* to squeeze blackheads.

7:05 Use product on hair. Lots of product. Begin flat iron process.

7:20 Squeeze blackheads.

7:30 Get mad at yourself for squeezing blackheads. Rush to makeup case. Try to erase red welts on your chin and forehead. Try to erase dark circles under your eyes. Try to erase entire face.

7:45 Get another Diet Coke. Tweeze eyebrows, hair on chin. Wonder why hair grows so quickly on every part of your body *except* your bangs.

7:46 Prepare home for that "I just got in" look. (See Date Decorating, page 75.)

8:00 Realize your hair is now too straight.

8:08 Wet hair, use curling gel, scrunch it dry.

8:10 Use curling iron to put back some of the curl.

8:20 Apply makeup.

8:40 Rip panty hose.

8:42 Try on turtleneck sweater, making sure to smudge mascara.

8:44 Reapply eye makeup.

8:50 Decide to wear slacks.

8:52 Speed-dress; try on every outfit in the closet. Pile discards on floor.

9:01 Apply seven layers of lipstick until your lips look like you're not wearing any lipstick.

9:05 Apply a quart of mousse to your hair for that natural look.

9:14   Test breath by breathing on hand.
9:15   Answer phone.
9:16   Listen to date.
9:20   Say, "No, no problem. Maybe we can do it another time."

getting ready for a date
in just over six minutes

A maneuver of such precision takes split-second timing and careful preparation. The night before this operation is set to take place, assemble all the required ingredients including perfume, deodorant, Binaca, blush-on, lip gloss, hairbrush, bourbon. Before you leave for work in the morning, align ingredients around bathroom sink, being careful to place things in the above order.

7:30   Arrive home and toss everything—coat, briefcase, mail, keys, umbrella, heels—on couch. Race to bathroom.
7:31   Spray perfume.
7:31:30   Roll on deodorant.
7:32   Spritz Binaca.
7:32:30   Wipe black crud from inside eyes and under bottom lid.
7:33   Apply blush to cheeks.
7:33:30   Apply gloss to lips.
7:34   Panic when doorbell rings.
7:34:30   Sweep brush through hair.
7:35   Check teeth for lunch leftovers.
7:35:30   Belt back bourbon.
7:36   Test breath by breathing on hand. Plaster smile on face.
7:36:30   Open door.

date decorating
preparing your home
for his arrival

For your first date with that special man, it is important to create the right impression. In other words, you want to present an image that will impress him, whether or not that image actually projects the real you. This may be a difficult concept for some women, especially those of us who came of age with mothers who were part of the baby boom generation in the late 1960s, early 1970s.

Mom told us over and over that looks didn't count, we were all beautiful human beings, what was on the inside was much more important than what was on the outside. Makeup is a mask, clothes don't make the woman. In hindsight, it's easy to recognize their mistake: we failed to take into account those principles applied only if you spent your formative years being stoned eighteen hours a day.[1]

Now that we know better, we need to update our standards to be more in keeping with modern times. This is why you must forget all that Be-Yourself, Take-Me-As-I-Am psychobabble that mom pounded into you. You are living in the material world. In the 2000s, you are what you mortgage.

Your living space says a lot about who you are and how you see yourself. Consequently, it is vital that your home project an image he will admire. This is no time to split hairs; if he thinks you're rich, he may find you even more attractive.

Projecting a successful image may take a lot of effort and time, depending on your bank account and on how much of a slob you really are. (This is something only you can honestly judge.) In all probability, however, you will have to spend at

---

1. As Grace Slick told *People* on August 28, 1978, "I stopped dropping acid for *awhile* [my italics] after my daughter was born. It's hard to keep an eye on the kid while you're hallucinating." Yeah, right, *that's* the generation who should be giving us advice. I don't think so.

least as much time getting your apartment together as you would yourself.

You want to really make this guy envious of your space, so here are a few of the steps you will need to take.

First, hide all evidence that you are frivolous, superficial, or just plain stupid. Remove from view: *People*, all your gossip/decorating/bridal magazines, astrology books, and/or *Hello Kitty* memorabilia.

Store all stuffed animals in the laundry hamper. (If this is too painful, send your furry friends on a sleepover with an understanding neighbor. While you're at it, deposit cat[s] and all their toys with the same neighbor. Remove all traces of kitty litter from sight and scent.)

Get rid of anything wicker, straw, gingham, or made of dried flowers or seashells. Hummels have to go. Knickknacks are definitely not 2000s.

Hide all CDs or tapes by whales (or any other marine life), Ricky Martin, Michael Bolton, or any *American Idol* participant (including winners, runner-ups, *and* judges). Remove any posters of Ashton Kutcher from walls, doors, or the refrigerator. Conceal those demented in-progress craft projects that you started but never finished.

Stock your refrigerator with cold cuts (late-night snack), lots of liquids, and breakfast (just in case).

Get out candles (but none that are carved into cute little animals or mushrooms). Stemmed candles that fit into candleholders only!

Buy yourself fresh flowers. If he asks who sent the flowers, be demure and smile. Then lie through your teeth. Say, "Just an old friend." Sigh deeply.

Hide Tampax and all other yucky personal hygiene items. You want him to think that, inside and out, you are put together as cleanly as a Barbie doll.

Try to be neat. Pick up all your dirty laundry and hide it under your bed. Stack dirty dishes in the oven or under the sink. For the sake of the entire female population, you always want to maintain the illusion that single women are not as messy as single men.

Overall, your apartment should be clean but not sterile. Unlike your mother, your date will not look under your couch for dust bunnies. (If he does, he should be dating your mother, not you.)

Strategically placed bits of clutter—an opened love letter here, an assortment of empty Tiffany boxes there—tells him you are orderly but not fanatic and, more important, that your life is interesting.

If you are doing well financially, don't keep it to yourself. Display your latest tax return on the coffee table. Leave some recent pay stubs and your stock portfolio on the dining room table.

A computer report that you lifted from the office tells him you're involved with your job. (If he asks about the printout, reply that you don't feel like "talking shop" tonight.)

Remember that first impressions are important. To ensure that he'll like you, don't be yourself. Be Charlize Theron.

the first date

Hallelujah!

Congratulations!

You've completed the two hardest tasks in the dating process:

1. You've found yourself a date.
2. You've found yourself something to wear.

You are about to embark on your first date, and you have plenty of reason to be excited. This is such a special time for you. The first date represents a wonderful moment in the dating process. This is when you and your date will develop your initial misconceptions about each other. Later on, if the relationship develops into something relatively permanent, you can look back to this time and cherish these first and lasting delusions.

But now is not the time to think about the future. You are about to face your next hurdle, and it's a big one. You must get through the first date in order to get on to the second date.

The first date is fraught with problems. Where will you go? How will you act? What will you talk about?

But let's cut to the chase here and discuss your biggest problem first.

sex on the first date

Should you have sex with him on the first date? If you have to ask (i.e., if that's not the sole reason for the date), then the answer is absolutely, unequivocally NO.

Researchers have calculated that the number of total dates you will have with a newfound man is directly proportionate to how many dates you wait until you have sex with him.

Sleep with a guy five minutes after you've met and your relationship will probably last as long as it takes him to lace up his Nikes.

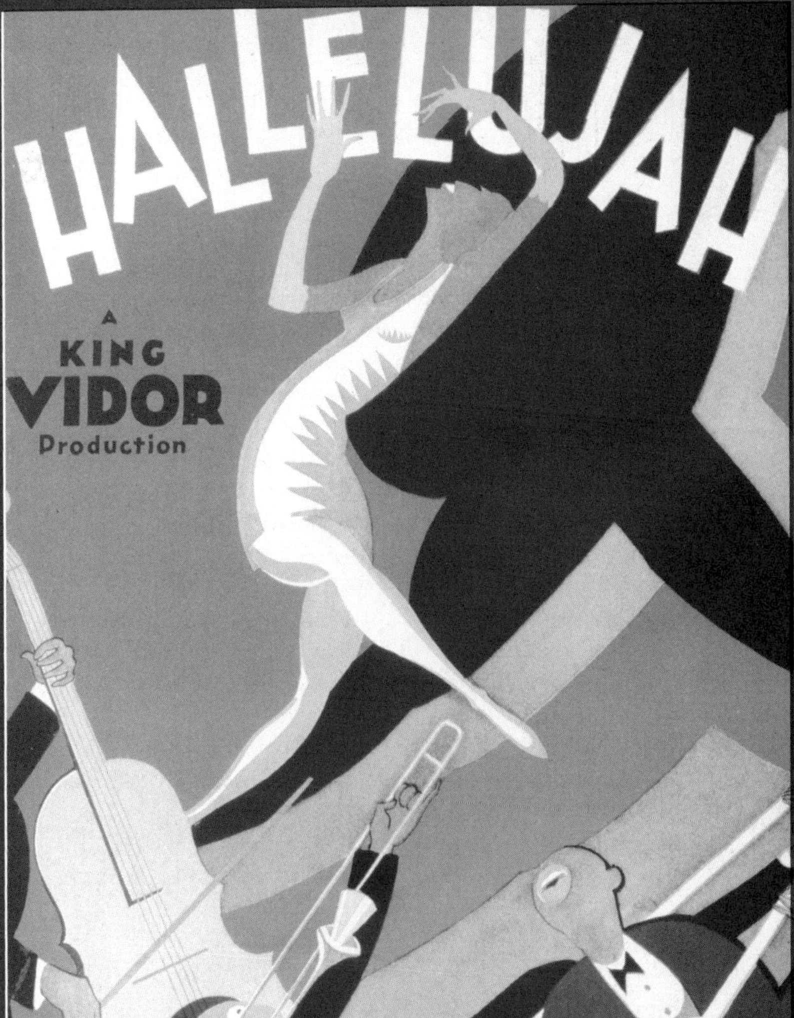
HALLELUJAH
A
KING
VIDOR
Production

Put the guy off until he's taken you to three movies, two plays, four museums, and three luncheons, and he's yours forever or until he decides to sleep with his secretary, his ex-wife, his ex-wife's sister, your sister, or a hairdresser named Enrique.

You must accept this: it is a proven fact that having sex on the first date is a mistake, *always*. Having sex on the first date practically guarantees that you'll never see the guy again for the following reasons:

a. If the sex is great—passionate, ecstatic, satisfying, no rope burns—he will immediately forget your last name, your telephone number, and everything else about you. It is unlikely that you will ever hear from him again.

b. If the sex is bad, you will not know each other well enough to get past the awkwardness in order to joke about the situation. He will be too embarrassed to call you again. Therefore, you will never get to the second date.

So, you see, you really cannot win.

Actually, none of this is new information. Since you were old enough to tell the difference between little girls and little boys, your mother has told you that it is always best to put a little mystery into a relationship, to hold off, and to realize that he won't buy the cow if there's always low-fat milk in the fridge. Well, the real shock is to discover that Mom was actually right about something.

Actually, the precedent goes back even further. In 1922, Helen Rowland, in her landmark book, *A Guide to Men: Reflections of a Bachelor Girl*, wrote: "It is no more reasonable to expect a man to love you tomorrow because he loves you today, than it is to assume that the sun will be shining tomorrow because the weather is pleasant today." Good point, Helen.

So, to reiterate once more:

RULE NUMBER 1: Do not have sex with him on your first date.

RULE NUMBER 2: After you've had sex with him on the first date, don't come crying to me (or your mother) when he doesn't call you again.

RULE NUMBER 3: Don't feel guilty for being human, you little slut.

where to go

Most couples prefer to go to the movies on a first date. This is a good way to spend time with another person and not have to make conversation.

You must be careful, however, in selecting a movie for the evening. You can tell a lot about a person from the kind of movies he or she likes to see. Make sure you make the right impression. Here are some simple guidelines:

a. Avoid any recent movie featuring Steve Martin or Martin Lawrence. You don't want to bore each other to death on your first date.

b. Avoid movies that were hailed in the reviews as misunderstood classics. I used to be a real sucker for reviews that began, "This is one of those rare films . . ." I've seen more of these movies than I care to admit, and, invariably, it's a mistake. Don't be fooled by precious quotes or precious reviewers. Almost anything with subtitles is also not great for a first date. You want your date to look at you during the course of the evening and not to have to concentrate so hard on the screen.

c. Avoid movies that are terrible, boring, and stupid, meaning any movie where cars, nerds, aliens, Kate Hudson, or Kevin Costner is given top billing.

d. Avoid, even more, movies that are terrible, boring, stupid, and violent, particularly such gems as *Dawn of the Dead*, *Van Helsing*, or anything remotely connected to *The Matrix*. (Of course, you probably already know never to see a movie starring Arnold Schwarzenegger or Steven Segal.)

e. Avoid movies that make you squirm in your seat. A General Rule of Thumb is to stay away from movies with any of the following words in their titles: *hot*, *hell*, *inches*, *kinky*, *nasty*, *peep*, *skin*, or *workout*.

f. A tip about romance movies: According to Dr. Joyce Brothers, it is better to go see a horror movie on a date than a romantic flick. The doctor says that romance movies are poor choices on a first date because they give your companion a comparison against which you'll never be able to compete. I guess the idea is that the uglier the actors on the big screen, the better your date will look to you here on earth. Therefore, don't go see Leonardo DiCaprio, Jude Law, Denzel Washington, Halle Berry, Catherine Zeta-Jones, or Reese Witherspoon in anything. If you're feeling real insecure, try an animated fish movie or a Michael Moore documentary.

what to eat

Never stay on your diet. Eat heartily. Don't pick at your food, and remember food is not to be played with. Do not burp loudly or otherwise embarrass your date. Do not ask for a doggie bag; you want him to think that you are never free to eat at home.

what drugs to take

Haven't you heard that drugs are out? Drinking is out. Smoking is out. Coffee is out. Carbs are out. Sex is out.

What's in? Money is in. Real estate is in. Investment banking is in.

About all that you can do with your date is to attend an Al-Anon meeting and, afterward, drink Perrier and discuss which mutual funds you have in common.

what to do

Here is a good game to play during the course of your first date. This game is the fastest way I know to slyly psychoanalyze a stranger, or as they used to say in simpler times, to get to know your date.

To play this game, you ask your date four seemingly innocent questions. Write down his answers. From these answers you will be able to glean a whole mass of subconscious, probably totally bizarre, fetishes belonging to your date.

Before you get to feeling too critical, however, it might be interesting for you to first answer these questions yourself and see what's barbecuing in your own subconscious backyard.

Be sure not to peek at the answers (i.e., the hidden meanings behind the questions) before you respond to the questions, or you'll ruin the game.

Remember (and remind your date), there are no "correct" answers to these questions. Try to respond as honestly as possible without thinking too much about how your answer will be interpreted.

Here are the four questions:

1. What is your favorite animal? Describe it in three adjectives.
2. What is your favorite color? Describe it in three adjectives.
3. What is your favorite body of water (i.e., ocean, lake, stream)? Describe it in three adjectives.
4. You are in an empty white room with no openings, doors, windows, or furniture. Describe how this makes you feel in three adjectives.

Hidden meanings:

1. His favorite animal indicates how he feels about himself. If he thinks of himself as a cute, cuddly, furry koala bear, he's probably a nice guy to be with on Sunday morning, though he might have a tendency to shed in warmer climates. If his favorite animal is a slimy, poisonous killer snake, your immediate reaction might be: Is there a back exit out of here?
2. His favorite color denotes the way he thinks others view him. If he describes his favorite color as warm, pleasing to the eye, and "great on a sofa," you'll know he isn't threatened by you. Take notice if he describes his favorite color as "penetrating" and/or "piercing." Trust me, he is trying to tell you something you do not want to know.
3. His favorite body of water is the most important category, because this is how he views sex. My last boyfriend selected the ocean and described it as eternal, foamy, and "smells good," which is as perfect a description of sex as I've ever come across. You might, however, want to be wary of the

guy who chooses a river because it's treacherous and the bottom is slimy and gooey.

4. Finally, the white room is symbolic of your date's feeling about death, and here we get into the really heavy psychological stuff. "Claustrophobic," "frightening," and "crazy" are not uncommon answers. Frankly, I've never heard an answer to this question that didn't seem totally appropriate except for a date who responded, "like the inside of a refrigerator" and "how much is the rent?"

what to discuss

After you've seen a movie, finished eating dinner, and played the above game, you will probably have to engage in some kind of conversation with your date. As we all know, this can be a terrifying prospect, especially if you've taken my advice and not gotten yourself stoned beyond comprehension. I have already discussed, in some detail, the topics of conversation to be avoided on a first date (see Speedy Dating, page 57). Here I just want to provide general guidelines. You want to appear intelligent, but you never want to let him know that you are smarter than him. Not that he would ever think that anyway. It is a basic mystery why a man cannot reconcile a woman's interest in shoes, makeup, and designer clothes with real brains while his own enthusiasm for golf clubs and baseball stats never seems, to him, incompatible with a superior intellect. Go know, as my aunt Hannah would always say.

Hopefully, the following guidelines may help you through the dreaded talking stage of your first date:

- If you talk about yourself, he'll think you're boring. If you talk about others, he'll think you're a gossip. If you talk about him, he'll think you are a brilliant conversationalist.

- Do not discuss bondage during the course of your conversation.

- Never whine on the first date.

- Try not to spend the entire evening asking yourself, Can I do better?

after the first date

debriefing guidelines

In government, all major missions of intrigue or danger are followed by a formal debriefing procedure. Astronauts, for example, are debriefed by NASA following their flights to the moon. The CIA and the Foreign Service insist upon debriefing hostages after their ordeal with their captors.

The debriefing procedure has relevance to the dating process because, as psychologists have noted, there are many similarities between the hostage situation and the first date. Specifically, both situations involve the unwilling participation of one of the parties involved and, usually, the sex isn't so great.

Consequently, many therapists now recommend a period of debriefing following the trauma of an initial encounter with a potential love object. Debriefing has proven useful to aid the single gal in clarifying the events of the evening as well as in easing her transition into being dateless again.

how to evaluate your first date

After he says good night (or good morning, if you've been naughty), sit down in a chair and review the events of the previous evening. Carefully reassess everything that went on during your date. Compile your "Date Data" by selecting from one of the two following scenarios:

SCENARIO A

Description: You and your date had absolutely nothing in common. You did nothing, in fact, but argue the entire evening.

He obviously felt antagonized by almost everything you said. You felt threatened every time he opened his mouth.

You felt he was not open to a relationship, he felt you were opinionated and hostile.

You were both convinced that the other person was hung up on a past relationship.

Conclusion: You can't wait to see him again.

Estimated Time for Him to Call for Another Date: Anywhere from one week to when hell freezes over.

Recommended Course of Action: Prepare yourself to sit around and wait for the phone to ring. Stock freezer with Häagen-Dazs and many frozen pizzas.

Supplemental Advice: Things to do while waiting for the phone to ring: knit, learn to tap dance, date someone else.

SCENARIO B

Description: You and your date got along well. You agreed about most things.

He listened to your opinions and gave careful consideration to what you said. He was attentive to your needs and eager to please you.

He stayed away from topics that made you uncomfortable or on which you obviously disagreed.

At the end of the evening, he asked if he could kiss you good night. Then he asked when (and if) he could call you for another date.

Conclusion: You never want to see him again.

Estimated Time for Him to Call for Another Date: Anywhere from one hour to two hours.

Recommended Course of Action: Keep calm. Try not to think less of him because he seems to really like you. If he calls to say how much he enjoyed himself on your date, do not get nervous and tell him to drop dead.

Keep in mind this important fact: his liking you a whole lot does not necessarily mean he is a moron.

In all probability, you will not want to date this guy again; you will, in fact, not want to live in the same city as him. If, however, you have not dated in a long, long time, you may want to reconsider your initial reaction. Remember it is possible that he can change. There's always the outside chance that he was only pretending to be a sweet, considerate guy. (Some guys are incredibly adept at faking sincerity and are known in psychiatric circles as the "Dr. Phil Impersonators.")

There's the remote possibility that, on your second date, he may completely stop being Mr. Nice Guy and start being seriously mean to you.

So, try to give the guy a break. Under his sensitive veneer may lurk the heart of a bastard; perhaps he'll even turn out to be the bastard of your dreams. Think what you'll be missing if you don't give him the opportunity to show his true self. After all, every guy deserves a fair chance to treat you like dirt.

post-debriefing

Once you are fully debriefed and have considered all your options in the wonderful world of dating, you may want to consider whether or not you wish to ever socialize again. Certainly, it is a tough game to play, and it may not surprise you to learn that it has always been difficult. Again, I quote from Helen Rowland who, in 1922, wrote: "To find your mate—that is luck; to know him when you find him—that is inspiration; to win him when you know him —that is art; and to keep him when you've won him—that is a *miracle.*" Helen wrote that more than eighty years ago, but can any modern woman dispute the wisdom of her observations?

an alternative to the first date

If you decide never to go out on another date, there is an alternative activity. You can easily simulate the feelings you have when you are with a date for the first time. You can do this without having to actually date anyone. The following situations will perfectly replicate the emotional experience of a first date:

GUYS: Sit on a hot radiator and tear up ten-dollar bills.

GALS: Stand naked on a busy street corner and pretend you're not embarrassed.

First dates are so much fun!
Now, are you ready for a relationship?

GRETA
GARBO
AS
YOU
DESIRE
ME
MELVYN DOU
ERICH VON STROH
OWEN MOORE
A
GEORGE
FITZMAURICE PRODUCTION
A
Metro-Goldwyn-Mayer Picture

sex

You will do foolish things,
but do them with enthusiasm.

COLETTE

What goes up must come down.
But don't expect it to come
down where you can find it.

JANE WAGNER,
*THE SEARCH FOR SIGNS OF
INTELLIGENT LIFE IN THE UNIVERSE,*
1986

what women want in bed

the width report

In 1976, a sexologist and statistician named Sheer Height shocked the nation by publishing a book on female sexuality that she modestly called *The Height Report*. The book reported the findings of a nationwide survey where women described their most intimate feelings about sex. *The Height Report* was hailed "as the best sex study since Masters and Johnson" (*The National Viewer*) and because, for many readers, ". . . it made us salivate!" (*The Beaver Observer*).

Obviously, Ms. Height's book captured the pulse of the female libido long before the first broadcast of *Sex and the City*. However, today's sexologists note that much has changed in the field of female sexuality since Ms. Height published her landmark book. For the past decade, women have been asking: Whatever happened to the sexual revolution? Why wasn't I invited?

Major events have altered the course of sexual patterns among singles. It's surely one of the strange phenomena of this decade that the most thoughtful gift you can bring a date is not flowers, chocolates, or ankle-length pearls, but a note from your doctor.

In order to chronicle these and other changes in women's sexual habits since the late 1970s, the publisher of this book financed a follow-up survey to *The Height Report*.

Sparing no expense, the publisher engaged the services of Dr. Claymore Width, PhD, from the McMasters Institute of Sexual Fantasies, an expert on female sexuality who was recently honored by *Star* magazine for his work in documenting female fantasies during intercourse. "Boy, you gals have dirty minds!" concluded the doctor.

After several months of research and development, Dr. Width finally completed a list of questions.

Just reading this questionnaire makes most women blush all over. In fact, the questions were so personal and intimate that Dr. Width's wife immediately sued for divorce, and his mistress, Muffy, left him. Even his dog, Scruffy, ran away from home.

The results of this survey will shock and disarm you. We discovered many discrepancies between our findings and those of Sheer Height. Naturally, we feel our report is far superior. At the McMasters Institute, where this report was painstakingly compiled, we remind ourselves: It's not the Height that counts, it's the Width!

findings from *the width report*

We questioned women in four basic areas of sexuality: masturbation, orgasm, sexual partners, and sexual acts.

The Height Report was probably one of the first books to openly discuss masturbation, and many people were shocked to even read that word in print. Remember, though, this was before Samantha Jones, when masturbation was still considered a subject most women didn't discuss with their parking lot attendant.

Contrary to *The Height Report*, we discovered that women were not as active in this area as Ms. Height implied in her book. On the subject of masturbation, women openly and freely gave us their honest answers. Responding to Dr. Width's question: *When you're all alone and feeling sexy, you would never, never, ever, do that nasty, disgusting, perverted thing to yourself, now would you?* Women reported:

"No! Never!"

"Of course not and how dare you ask that?"

"What do I look like, a psychopath?"

"No, Mommy, I swear, cross my heart."

Having dispelled that myth, Dr. Width went on to question women about their personal relationship to orgasms.

Sexologists like Dr. Width have known for years that the ways in which women experience orgasms are varied. Dr. Width asked: *How do you know when you achieve orgasm?*

His questions asked women to describe, in detail, what it felt like when they achieved orgasm during sex (in the missionary position and only for the purposes of procreation, of course). The responses turned out to be as varied as the women themselves.

"I go gushy all over and then I break out in hives."

"My body tenses completely and I levitate toward Mecca."

"I go completely motionless. I almost stop breathing. Once my husband gave me artificial respiration because he thought I'd died."

"I scream 'Praise the Lord' and then start singing 'The Chipmunk Song.'"

"I get a nosebleed."

"I vibrate, moan, have seizures, scream, claw, pant, have contractions, shudder, shiver, lose control of my pelvis, grab my partner's buttocks—and that's only for the first orgasm. By the tenth or eleventh, I really go crazy!"

"What's an orgasm?"

As much as women obviously enjoy orgasm, *The Width Report* reveals an important new element in understanding how women feel about sex. In the past, sexual discussions almost always centered around orgasms. It seemed, in fact, that the single most important component of sex, for women, was orgasm. However, in this new survey, Dr. Width discovered that female sexuality today is not just a matter of achieving orgasm. The twenty-first-century woman wants more, much more! Here, then, Dr. Freud, is what women really want:

"It's not just orgasm I'm interested in. I also want a toaster oven."

". . . a Dustbuster."

". . . TiVo!"

"My boyfriend makes wild, passionate love to me and then rolls over and goes to sleep. This makes me crazy. After sex, I want him to give me a home perm."

". . . tweeze my eyebrows."

". . . fix the leaky faucet in the bathroom."

"Why can't men be more considerate? I'd like my lover to think about my feelings and my needs. Just once, after he comes, he could stay awake long enough to help me polish the silverware."

The Width Report attempted to determine women's preferences in their choice of sex partners. Unfortunately, however, we could not get a scientifically accurate reading in response to our question on this subject because, for some unknown reason, Dr. Width's question about sex partners confused most of the women who responded to the questionnaire. Perhaps the question was not written clearly enough, although no one at McMasters had any trouble understanding the doctor's intention when he asked: *With whom would you prefer to have sex?*

a. Keanu Reeves

b. Viggo Mortensen

c. Your washing machine

d. Fresh produce

Instead of answering this multiple-choice question, many women responded with questions of their own. They asked the doctor to clarify certain points:

"Who's Keanu Reeves?"

"*The Fellowship of the Rings*, *The Two Towers*, or *Return of the King*?"

"Which cycle, rinse or spin dry?"

"Steamed or raw?"

Overall, however, those who understood the question voted overwhelmingly for the fresh produce, especially if it came with guacamole dip.

Dr. Width's next multiple-choice question asked women to select their favorite sexual act. Due to certain copyright laws and the publisher's definition of what constitutes pornography, we are not allowed to reprint the specific choices of sexual acts that Dr. Width offered in this question.[1] However, the results of this question, in terms of which sex *act* women pre-

---

1. Note to the public: This question was specifically cited in Dr. Width's divorce hearing, and, after it was read aloud in open court, Mrs. Width was awarded custody of the children, the house, the CD collection, and everything Dr. Width had ever touched without rubber gloves.

fer, confirmed that the majority of women preferred answer (d), intercourse with a human being.

These responses constitute the major findings of *The Width Report*.[2] In all, the questionnaire was mailed to more than four million women in the continental United States. Answers were tabulated from the thirteen women who responded.

Wondering why so many of these women took the time and effort to read through this gargantuan questionnaire, the institute called each and every one and asked why they'd bothered to respond. Their answers varied:

"It's time women spoke out about sex!"

"I was under the dryer with nothing else to do."

"I was too young to get in on *The Height Report*, so I'm real glad I had another opportunity."

"Answering this questionnaire got me hot!"

"My husband made me do it while he watched."

There are many conclusions that can be drawn from the results of *The Width Report*, not the least of which is whether Dr. Width should be allowed to continue practicing medicine. But the overall response to this questionnaire has led Dr. Width and his colleagues at the institute to conclude that women today feel that, in the best of all possible worlds, sex would be something they could enjoy without always getting asked to answer questionnaires all the time.

"Wouldn't it be great if we just did it, instead of getting tested all the time?" wrote one housewife from Des Moines. "I get six or seven questionnaires a week; there's hardly enough room in my mailbox for all the junk mail from Bed, Bath and Beyond and Walgreens. What I want to know is, When am I going to actually get paid for all this information? Sheer Height made a bundle on her book, but did I see a single dime for all my work? No. It ain't fair. Talk about getting screwed!"

2. For readers who are interested, a more detailed assessment is available through the McMasters Institute for an unbelievably exorbitant fee.

take this test

am i a good lover, or what?

Are you a good lover, or what?

This is a question that can only partially be answered by you alone. Your Significant Other probably has a pretty knowledgeable opinion on the subject, so you should take this test together.

Score five points every time you and your Significant Other agree on an answer.

If you don't have a lover, take the test twice and see how well you get along with yourself.

1. The most important factor in a relationship is:
   a. mutual respect
   b. compatible astrology signs
2. My favorite fragrance is:
   a. Vera Wang for Women
   b. Windex
3. If your lover suggests using a condom during intercourse, would you ask:
   a. "What's a condom?"
   b. "What's intercourse?"
4. When your lover does something during sex that turns you off, you:
   a. pretend to enjoy it to spare his feelings
   b. scream, "STOP THAT!!!"
5. You use sex as:
   a. a reward
   b. a punishment
6. Your current Significant Other enjoys sex:
   a. with the lights on
   b. with someone else
7. Your preferred method of birth control is:
   a. to use a diaphragm
   b. to mention marriage

8. The idea of oral sex makes you:
   a. salivate
   b. regurgitate
9. An unmade bed describes:
   a. your favorite playing field
   b. the way he looks in clothes
10. The last person who sent you flowers was:
    a. your Significant Other
    b. the dinner guest who got sick all over your bathroom floor
11. Sex with a total stranger is:
    a. immoral
    b. your definition of marriage
12. Who wrote the book of love?
    a. Ben Affleck
    b. your accountant
13. When your lover doesn't get aroused, you:
    a. say, "That's okay, honey. Let's try tomorrow."
    b. pick up the phone and call someone else
14. You believe love:
    a. makes the world go round
    b. is as good an excuse as any
15. Your sex life is:
    a. your business
    b. everybody's business
16. During sex you think about:
    a. your lover
    b. your doorman
17. For a romantic date, you'd serve a bottle of:
    a. French Champagne
    b. Viagara
18. Home is where:
    a. your heart is
    b. you do your laundry
19. You don't need a lot of money because:
    a. you have your health
    b. you have your credit cards

20. You like having money because:
    a. you can help others
    b. you're hard on shoes
21. Your most erogenous zone is:
    a. in the crook your neck
    b. in the frozen foods department
22. You need sex:
    a. every day
    b. every leap year
23. You are really impressed if your lover:
    a. goes out of his way to please you
    b. wants to know your address
24. Your ideal date is with:
    a. Russell Crowe
    b. Hillary Duff

OPTIONAL QUESTIONS

25. Why are you taking this test?
    a. It's here
    b. You hope to improve yourself
26. If a test told you to jump out of the window, would you do it?
    a. No
    b. Only if it would make my breasts bigger

SCORING

75–125: You and your lover are really compatible. You see eye to eye on almost everything. You have a lot in common and are perfectly suited for each other. I give your relationship one week.

45–70: You and your lover share the basic ingredients necessary for a satisfying sexual relationship. You agree on some of the most important things and are therefore relatively compatible. If one of you has a lot of money, your relationship has potential.

0–40: Obviously, you two have absolutely nothing in common, which means you are incredibly hot together. Be forewarned that you are in serious danger of a fatal attraction that may result in a long-term commitment. Proceed with extreme caution.

OPTIONAL QUESTIONS: If you answered either of these questions, deduct fifty points from your test score. Go to the nurse's office and get a pass to go home. You are suffering severe test stress. You need to cut down immediately. You are absolutely forbidden to read *Vanity Fair* for the next six months.

sex ruins everything
a true-life confession

My friend Carol says that every eligible man should have an expiration date stamped on his forehead, like a carton of milk. "That way you'd know just how long he's going to last before turning sour on you."

Unfortunately, love (and I hesitate to use the word) doesn't come with any directions or boundaries or instructions (and forget the idea of a warranty altogether). Past experience doesn't help much either because, even though you keep making the same mistakes over and over again, you make them with different men, so they *seem* like different mistakes.

Larry the dentist is a case in point, or just a case, as the point may be. I thought he really liked me. I mean, really, really liked me. And I liked the way he liked me, so we went out a couple of times. He talked about me meeting his friends. He told me I was gorgeous. He said he liked talking to me; he was interested in my ideas. Once he said, "I'm nervous because I really want you to like me." I told him that, in general, I was skeptical about the possibility of having a relationship in my life. He said, in general, he was eternally optimistic. We talked about his family, my family, friends, long-gone relationships, the recent past.

Secondhand confirmation arrived from the mutual friend who'd introduced us. She said: "He said you were perfect. He said he could get lost in your hair. He said he wanted to invite you to Vermont for the weekend."

He wrote me a poem: "I remember the days when I couldn't remember the sights smells sounds of you. But today, the calmness belies the spinning and twirling of emotions—a merry-go-round of love."

I was flattered, enchanted, charmed. He was in my thoughts. I began to think that, maybe, this might work out. A long shot, of course, but once you let that nasty optimism in the door, all kinds of possibilities come rushing in.

One night, after dinner, we were sitting in my apartment and he kissed me lightly, on the lips. It was a passing gesture. He continued talking. I leaned over and kissed him. "I really wanted to kiss you," I said. Buttons came undone and silent zippers, too. He went into the kitchen to get me a glass of water. I remember the ice-cold water in my mouth and the sight of him standing at my bedroom door, beckoning me with a crooked finger and a wrinkly smile.

Two days later, he called late at night. "You know I want to be really honest with you. I don't have casual sex or get involved in casual relationships, so I don't think we should have sex again. Not that I'm not attracted to you, or anything, but I just don't see our relationship going in that direction. Of course, I still want to see you again. I'm kind of busy for the weekend, so why don't we have dinner next Tuesday night?"

I played with this conversation, over and over, in the next few days, wondering how I could turn it around so it didn't sound so much like I was getting dumped because I had had sex with him. I tried to concoct a scenario where he was backing off because he liked me so much he was scared, but even I had to admit that the concept was full of holes.

I thought and thought. I analyzed. Actually, I obsessed.

What did he mean by casual sex? Did he mean sex without the possibility of commitment? Or did he define casual sex as sex with someone he didn't want to have sex with again? Or, even worse, did he relate to my friend's definition: "Casual sex is sex with someone you don't really like."

I felt bad. He didn't want to have sex with me again so, of course, I desperately wanted to have sex with him, which raises the eternal dating dichotomy: Why would you want someone who doesn't want you?

I'd completely tossed aside the fact that I'd had genuine doubts about him. When we first met, I described my feelings about him to my friends like this: "Well, we have no future, but we could have a great present." After all, we were really different. He was too young, too conventional, and too conservative for me. He played golf, I went to the movies. He got up at the crack of dawn, I never went to sleep before three a.m. His philosophy of life was "Excess in moderation." Mine was "Fantasy over reality, any day."

So, if I knew all that, why was I feeling so bad? Well, of course, I told myself, it all had to do with my childhood and my mother and my sense of self-esteem and all those other buzzwords. Oh, please, I thought, don't let this turn into another one of life's lessons that I needed to learn. (I'm so tired of growing as a person.) I decided that I was causing myself to feel bad, and, therefore, I could also cause myself to feel better. So I began to look for reasons to feel positive.

For a while, I appreciated that he'd been so honest with me. After all, I told myself, there are lots of guys who never tell you what they're thinking or feeling and you only figure it out after you haven't heard from them in three or four months. But then this appreciation faded when I realized his honesty would have been a lot more helpful if he had expressed his doubts *before* we had sex.

I decided to focus on this problem: BS (Before Sex), I had invited him to a formal party for the following week. AS (After Sex), he called to make arrangements for the party. I hemmed and hawed, having a hard time saying what was in my heart, which was essentially this: "I'm really confused about what went down between us in such a short time, I don't think we should go to this party together, and I hope your dick falls off and you die a miserable death."

I stammered out the part about not going to the party but held back on the rest of the speech because, in my heart of hearts, I was hoping that he'd argue with me and talk me out of disinviting him to the party. (Then I wouldn't want him dead, or dickless, for that matter.) Not that I needed to worry. He didn't fulfill my fantasy. In fact, he relented rather easily, expressing regret mainly about missing an opportunity to wear his expensive new tux.

I know (well, I suspect) that if I hadn't had sex with him, we would've gone to that party and had a wonderful time. We would've had, probably, several more dinners, lots of phone conversations. Maybe I would've met his friends, maybe he would've met some of mine. Maybe he would've written me more poetry that scanned better. Then again, maybe this is me going off on another fantasy because, inevitably, we would've had sex and, I'm quite sure, AS, the same situation.

Anyway, here's my major observation about this embarrassing episode in my dating career, and I'm going to italicize it because I may have uncovered the major difference between men and women: *I had doubts about him before we had sex; he had doubts about me after we had sex.*

Translation: Sex eliminates a good many doubts for women. Or, I should say, good sex compensates for having to wrestle with a few doubts. And, undeniably, having a man inside you changes you. This totally confuses men. I don't think they can begin to understand how sex internalizes a woman's feelings, fusing the physical with the emotional.

And, not understanding, men get confused. They withdraw.

So, sex ruins everything. After it makes you feel good, it makes you feel possessive and mean and mad. It shatters your fantasies. It clouds your judgment and destroys your reason. It makes you turn every minor incident into a major experience. It makes everything seem lopsided. It takes a nice evening and turns it into a potential battlefield. It makes you long for feelings that aren't there. It makes you crazy, and it breaks your heart.

When Larry called and I told him we shouldn't go to the party, I also said, "Sex ruins everything." He said if I wrote a book with that title, it would sell a million copies.

Instead I wrote this chapter, and curious about how Larry would react, I sent him a copy. He called and said, "You've really captured what happened between us very accurately except for one glaring problem. I think you're confusing sex with love."

Of course I am. That's what women do, you moron, and what's more, we do not understand why men don't. If you could write a book explaining how men can separate love from sex, I want to tell Larry, you could sell ten million copies.

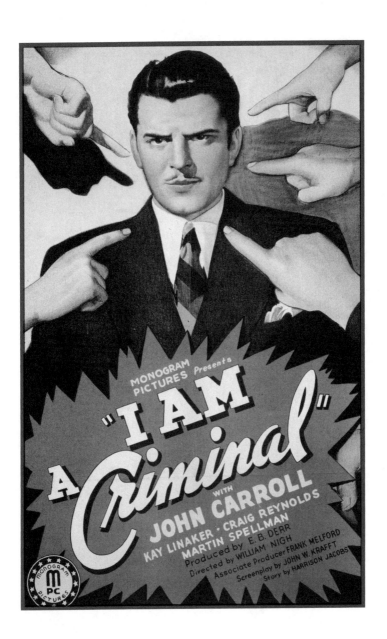

relationships

Gertrude loved with all the
delusion of romance, and, like
many a young enthusiast, had
mistaken her imagination
for her mind.

SUSAN FERRIER,
THE INHERITANCE,
1824

Delusions of grandeur make me
feel a lot better about myself.

JANE WAGNER

what is a healthy relationship?

What constitutes a healthy relationship between a man and a woman? This question has plagued singles since the invention of the Sock Hop.

The concept of a healthy relationship was first described in 1983 by the German psychiatrist Dr. Zigfried Frung in his landmark paper, *What Makes Dick and Jane Run Together?*

"In the healthy relationship," claimed Dr. Frung, "you will not spend more than fifteen minutes per evening worrying that your friends will think less of you when they meet your date."

Previous to the publication of Dr. Frung's paper, it was generally accepted that a healthy couple didn't fight all the time. "This is simply not true," stated Dr. Frung. "A healthy couple fights about every insignificant detail and then has great sex. In an unhealthy relationship, the couple fights about every insignificant detail *during* sex."

In writing about sex, Dr. Frung makes frequent reference to the work of Masters and Johnson and Johnson, a team of psychiatrists who gained fame in the late 1960s for their work with ménage à trois relationships.

"In a healthy relationship between only two people," wrote Masters and Johnson and Johnson, "you do not wake up in the mornings wondering, How quickly can I get this person out of my apartment?

"This rule of thumb is, however, mitigated if, before you've brushed your teeth or had a cup of coffee, your date says, 'I think I'm insulted by what you said last night' and expects you to care."

According to Dr. Frung's observations, sexual compatibility in a healthy relationship is strengthened if both partners realize that compromise is essential. The real paradox for today's singles is that they spend the greater part of their adult lives refining and improving themselves to the point of perfection and then have to compromise to keep their love object (who was the reason they wanted to be perfect in the first place). "People would love to take the *settle* out of settle down," said Masters, "but it don't work that way."

Many of Frung's early observations have survived virtually intact and are as fresh as this morning's newspaper headlines. For example, a major theme of Dr. Frung's work is the concept of Dating Down. "In a healthy relationship," he wrote, "the man dates up the social ladder and the woman dates down. This changes radically for men after marriage. Married men always date down after their wedding vows. Married women, however, continue in their previous pattern by dating their personal trainers and car mechanics."

The proof of Dr. Frung's observation was recently verified by President Clinton, who is a textbook example of someone who married up and yet dated down, many times.

Dr. Frung maintains that the American public was first exposed to a healthy relationship on the popular television show *Will and Grace*, which proved that the best relationship a girl can ever hope to have is with a good-looking, intelligent, and witty gay man.

Dr. Frung's theories on the existence of a healthy relationship have not gone uncontested. A conflicting body of opinion maintains there is no such thing as a healthy relationship. Dr. Juend, one of the major opponents of the healthy relationship concept, argues, "Most couples aren't really in love, they just act that way to aggravate their single friends."

Apparently, most singles in today's dating pool question the very existence of the so-called healthy relationship.

In a recent Harrison poll, when asked for a definition of a healthy relationship, most singles replied, "Duh?"

In fact, many people cannot psychologically accept the rigors of such arrangements. "I've tried healthy relationships," claims thirty-seven-year-old bachelor Hawk Zipkin, "but, I don't know, I feel more comfortable in a neurotic situation. I think severe psychological humiliation and daily traumatic assaults on my masculinity make life more interesting. Don't you?"

In an article for *Cosmo*, Dr. Frung advised readers about the two specific feelings that signal the onset of an unhealthy relationship.

1. The feeling that you've lowered your standards beyond a "reasonable" amount.
2. After your first evening together, the only definitive conclusion you've reached is that you would've had a better time alone, even in bed.

Getting through the "Firsts" without suffering a massive anxiety attack is one of Dr. Frung's main criteria for forming a healthy relationship. For example, after spending your first night together, you should not consider it an unfair obligation to make your date a cup of coffee in the morning. The other important such Firsts, as noted by Dr. Frung, include the First Shower Together, First Full Weekend, First Party with His Friends, First Dinner with Your Friends, First Time You Cook for Him, and the First Pregnancy Scare.

case study

In the *Grimness Book of World Records*, the world's longest running healthy relationship began in 1980 when Tom Bitterman, a high school freshman from Terre Haute, Indiana, asked out Florence Barclay, a born-again cheerleader, also of Terre Haute. The two became instantly inseparable. Within a week, they'd invented pet names for each other.

The Tom and Florence Phenomenon, as it was later called in psychiatric circles, was, according to Dr. Frung, "so normal that it was disgusting."

Tom and Florence used baby talk to communicate with each other, often inflicting this revolting language on their friends.

The couple constantly referred to themselves as "we," although, when separated, Tom mentioned Florence's name twenty-six times a day and Florence managed to refer to "my boyfriend" a whopping thirty-three times.

They began to dress alike, favoring plaid flannel shirts and matching scarves. On campus they were known as Ken and Barbie.

Tom claimed to love Florence's mother.

The couple scored 99 percent on every *Cosmo* compatibility test they ever took together.

In restaurants, Tom ordered Florence's meals; she cut his meat.

Tom bought Florence so much candy that, in one college semester, she gained twenty-five pounds, as did her roommate. Tom thought Florence looked cute carrying the extra weight and he took to calling her "my pudgy wudgy." He begged her not to lose an ounce.

The couple waited approximately eight years, until they were married, to have sex.

At their tenth high school reunion, Tom Bitterman announced that his marriage "was still a bowl of cherries. We were never happier. No man alive could ask for a better wife than my little Florie-Dorie."

"Oh, Flubby-Dub," cooed Florence.

Enraged, the crowd of fellow classmates (who were mostly divorced and/or desperately single) jeered the Bittermans off the dance floor. Two months later, alumni from the Class of 1984 voted unanimously to blackball Tom and Florence from all future high school reunions. Their names were permanently stricken from the yearbook. Tragically, they were retroactively impeached as king and queen of the senior prom.

Neighbors in Terre Haute began to shun the ever-smiling couple. The Bitterman home was bombarded with phony phone calls, nasty letters, and rotten eggs. One night, a group of neighbors, dressed in white sheets, defaced the Bitterman home with the four cruelest words in the English language. Across the two-car garage, the angry crowd painted the slogan, "Have a Nice Day!" A week later, the mob returned and fire-burned a smiling Happy Face on the Bittermans' front lawn.

After the Bittermans' appeal for state protection was denied by the governor (who was, coincidentally, a college acquaintance of Tom's and a bitter, twice-divorced father of six), they were forced to sell their house and move to another state. Under a federal protection program, the Bittermans are now living under an assumed name, posing as an unhappily married couple who attend counseling three times a week.

What Dr. Frung failed to acknowledge in his paper was that the healthy relationship can pose a serious threat of jealous rage, provoking otherwise peace-loving friends and neighbors to acts of violence—certainly one of the main reasons why healthy relationships are so rare in today's society.

> The man she had was kind and clean
> And well enough for every day,
> But, oh dear friends, you should've seen
> The one that got away!
>
> —DOROTHY PARKER,
> *DEATH AND TAXES*, 1931

nice guys vs. bad boys

Single women should know that, in the whole universe, there are only two kinds of men: Nice Guys and Bad Boys. And, it is a general rule of thumb that we date nice guys but we fall for bad boys.

Let's face it, men make us nuts, but here's the rub: we resent when Nice Guys drive us crazy, but when Bad Boys drive us crazy, we think it's love.

Ever wonder why, in the dating game, nice guys always finish last? The answer is revealed in the following chart:

nice guys	bad boys
Calls every day *Score: –10 for being desperate*	**Calls once every 2 weeks** *Score: +10 for ever calling*
Always compliments you *–10 for making you feel uncomfortable*	**Never notices new haircut** *+10 for staying in your comfort zone*
Brings you roses *–10 for making you feel guilty for accepting gifts*	**Never promised you a rose garden** *+10 for honesty*
Makes date 2 weeks in advance *–10 for being too available*	**Calls at last minute** *+10 for being popular*
Has steady job (accountant, dentist, etc.) *–10 for being ordinary*	**Unemployed** *+10 for creativity, being artistic, antiestablishment*
Wants to meet your family *–10 for being toady*	**Doesn't want to be with your family** *+10 because neither do you*
Wants to meet your best friend *–10 for trying to worm his way into your life and not giving you space*	**Wants to date your best friend** *+10 for making you feel jealous, which also feels like love*

nice guys {continued}

Wants a serious relationship
−10 for not finding one

Works hard to please you
−10 for being dependent

Takes you to expensive restaurants
−10 for making you wear panty hose

Extremely interested in your work
−10 for asking too many questions

Talks about his feelings
−10 because his feelings are never in sync with yours

Tells you when to dress casual for a date
−10 for always wearing geeky jeans

Tells stupid jokes
−10 for boredom

Bonus Points
+ 10 for always driving a nice car

bad boys {continued}

Can't make a commitment
+10 for being a challenge

Only pleases you when he feels like it
+10 for independence

Wants you to cook for him
+10 for eating your food

Extremely interested in his work
+10 for making you into a good listener

Never discusses his feelings
+10 for allowing you to fantasize how he feels about you

Doesn't care about clothes
+10 for looking great naked

Tells stupid jokes
+10 for making you laugh

+250 for always being a great kisser

total score:

NICE GUYS: −130

BAD BOYS: +390

any questions?

dear dating maven

answers to reader e-mail

Advice is cheap but Botox costs a fortune so, for a while, I paid my plastic surgeon with income derived from an "advice to the lovelorn" type Web site that I ran out of my house. The site did quite well, and for several months, I had a forehead that was as smooth as glass. I enjoyed answering reader e-mails and thought I had a real talent for telling them where (and how) to get off. I used my own life experiences to guide my readers through the treacheries of dating.

One day I wrote an anecdotal story about a high school acquaintance of mine who I shall call Miss XXX, as the courts have ruled that I can no longer mention her name. Miss XXX was always mean to me. In sixth grade, she started a hate club against me when I forgot to save her seat on the first day of class, and our friendship never really recovered. Miss XXX also had the most perfect, honey blonde hair that curled into a glorious ponytail, so there were other reasons, beside the hate club incident, to dislike her.

One day, in my column, I related to my readers a bit of high school gossip about Miss XXX that involved Mr. Schmidt, our drama coach, who cast Miss Perfect Ponytail, over me, for the lead in *My Fair Lady*. The rumor involved the way she had snatched Eliza from my more deserving hands and the acrobatic feats she had employed in Mr. Schmidt's private office to achieve her goal. Well, long story short, she sued me. The Bitch.

I was ordered to shut down my site and pay her a ridiculous settlement that she later told the press would keep her in Manolo Blahniks for years to come.

All this, just because I called her a "good-time girl with a bad-time rep," which I thought was not only appropriate but a nice turn of phrase. Of course, it came out in court that the person who had started the rumor in high school was me, and my lawyer advised that I settle as quickly as possible.

So, now my crow's feet are snaking their way down to my ears. But, when I was still active, I know I helped many readers. I really excel at telling people what to do. I've had years and years of experience. Ask anyone who knows me, especially my sister.

The following is from my e-mail archives and, I think, proves the point that the world lost a valuable resource when Miss Ponytail walked into the courtroom.

TO: DATINGMAVEN@NOTAREALADDRESS.COM
FROM: CORA@ALOSS.COM

Dear Dating Maven,

I have a problem with my boyfriend, Jeff. He's always talking about how much he hates himself. He says that if I break up with him, he'll really go berserk. Sometimes he talks about killing himself. In fact, I spent most of our last date talking him in off the window ledge.

His behavior has taken the romance out of the relationship, and I'm thinking about not seeing him anymore. But then I wonder: Should I take all this suicide stuff seriously?

Also, if I dump Jeff, will I be able to find another date for my sister's wedding?

CORA

TO: CORA@ALOSS.COM
FROM: DATINGMAVEN@NOTAREALADDRESS.COM

Dear Cora,

It's difficult to fully analyze your situation considering you did not provide me with a great deal of information. In order to properly advise you, I need answers to the following questions: How much does Jeff earn a year? Is he husband material? And, what are your chances of attracting a new guy? What is the condition of your inner thighs?

Suicide is serious business and needs careful deliberation. The loss of any single man reduces the odds of getting married for every single female.

DATING M.

TO: DATINGMAVEN@NOTAREALADDRESS.COM
FROM: CORA@ALOSS.COM

Dear Dating M,
Jeff is an unemployed mime performer with a serious drinking problem. Also, he likes to dress up like a French maid and dust my bookshelves.

I am a sales rep for a major pharmaceutical company and I support both of us.

I jog ten to twenty miles a day. My inner thighs have been compared to aluminum siding.

CORA

TO: CORA@ALOSS.COM
FROM: DATINGMAVEN@NOTAREALADDRESS.COM

Dear Cora,
Open your windows and wear a miniskirt to the office.

DM

TO: DATINGMAVEN@NOTAREALADDRESS.COM
FROM: CORA@ALOSS.COM

Dear DM,
All through Jeff's funeral, I kept wondering: Why do my relationships always end badly? I really do want to get seriously involved with a man. What am I doing wrong?

I was nuts about my boyfriend before Jeff. His name was Tony and he was such a great guy that I didn't even mind when he'd ask me to scoop up after his Great Dane.

When Tony left me for his brother's ex-second wife, I stayed in bed for ten days and cried myself a river.

How can I avoid getting hurt like this again?

CORA FROM DETROIT

Dear Cora,

There's a simple solution to your dating dilemma. Only date men you don't like.

Actually, the more repulsive, the better.

This way, when they dump you, you will not care.

D. MAVEN

Dear D. Maven,

I took your advice and now I'm dating a man I can't stomach.

Dick is a successful periodontist who insists that we floss before sex. He's an awful dresser and I really hate his hair.

Dick and I have been seeing each other for almost two months, and if he ever decides to dump me, I'll thank my lucky stars.

Dick's thirty-fifth birthday is next week and I don't know what to get him. The only gift he claims to want is an "official" Star Trek uniform. When I ask him why he wants such a thing he blushes and can't give me a reason.

Don't you think he's a little old for this? What am I to make of his request?

NOT A TREKKIE

Dear Not A Trekkie,

What rank uniform does Dick want?

DM

Dear DM,

Science Officer.

Leonard Nimoy (Mr. Spock) is like a god to Dick.

CORA

TO: CORA@ALOSS.COM
FROM: DATINGMAVEN@NOTAREALADDRESS.COM

Dear Cora,
Any rank lower than Captain is unacceptable.

DATING MAVEN

TO: DATINGMAVEN@NOTAREALADDRESS.COM
FROM: CORA@ALOSS.COM

Dear Dating Maven,
Dick hated the electric shaver I bought him for his birthday and we broke up a week later.

I was thrilled to have him out of my life, but I still really want to get married. I mean, I really want to get married. What can I do?

GUESS WHO?

TO: CORA@ALOSS.COM
FROM: DATINGMAVEN@NOTAREALADDRESS.COM

Dear Cora,
Do not despair. There is a huge, untapped pool of men who will not only marry you but who'll pay you $5,000 for the privilege. These men are called immigrants or aliens (but are not the kind found on the Starship Enterprise).

These available men need to marry a woman of your obvious social position (i.e., American) in order to get their green cards and stay in this country.

Although these marriages are often belittled as "marriages of convenience," single women know that marriage to anyone is always more convenient than being single.

To find an immigrant, you can hang out in Chinatown or visit a Third World country. Good luck!

DM

TO: DATINGMAVEN@NOTAREALADDRESS.COM
FROM: CORA@ALOSS.COM
Dear Dating Maven,
My new boyfriend and I saw you on Dr. Phil's show last week.
Juan Jose thought you were "muy bueno" and I thought you were
very good, too.
  I couldn't help notice the huge diamond on your finger. I told
Juan Jose the ring had to be a fake, right?

CORA

TO: CORA@ALOSS.COM
FROM: DATINGMAVEN@NOTAREALADDRESS.COM
Dear Cora,
The only thing that's fake about me are my tits, my tan, my nose,
my lips, my front teeth, and my feelings about my sister-in-law.

DM

TO: DATINGMAVEN@NOTAREALADDRESS.COM
FROM: CORA@ALOSS.COM
Dear Dating Maven,
I travel a lot on my job so I'm separated several nights a week
from my husband. How can I tell if Juan Jose is unfaithful to me?

CONCERNED IN DETROIT

TO: CORA@ALOSS.COM
FROM: DATINGMAVEN@NOTAREALADDRESS.COM
Dear Concerned,
If your husband is very affectionate (especially around other peo-
ple) and if he always wants to make love, you can generally
assume that he is fooling around with another woman. On the
other hand, I wouldn't complain if I were you.

DATING MAVEN

TO: DATINGMAVEN@NOTAREALADDRESS.COM
FROM: CORA@ALOSS.COM

Dear Dating Maven,

Juan Jose and I divorced about six months ago. (I left him for my male secretary.) We had no children so we don't get to see each other at all anymore.

The problem is that I think I still love my Juan Jose and he told my mother that he still loves me. I would like to build a new relationship with him but I'm embarrassed after all the verbal abuse we flung at each other in divorce court.

Should I try seeing him again?

EX-SEÑORA

TO: CORA@ALOSS.COM
FROM: DATINGMAVEN@NOTAREALADDRESS.COM

Dear Ex-Señora,

Dating A.D. (After Divorce), especially an ex-husband, is very difficult business and should be considered only if you haven't had any sex in a very long time, which, from the sound of your office situation, is not the case.

However, in your favor is that you are also Dating B.C. (Before Children), which does make it easier because there are no witnesses if you make a fool of yourself.

Why not call your ex and feel him out? Better yet, drop by where he works. It's always better to feel someone out in person.

DM

TO: DATINGMAVEN@NOTAREALADDRESS.COM
FROM: CORA@ALOSS.COM

Dear DM,

I hardly get any sleep at all anymore. Baby Maven Jose is up all night screaming.

What can I do about severe diaper rash?

CORA

TO: CORA@ALOSS.COM

FROM: DATINGMAVEN@NOTAREALADDRESS.COM

Dear Cora,

Sorry, diaper rash is Ann Landers's domain. Kisses to Baby Maven.

DM

dating younger men

Let's get personal for a minute. What are we to really think of dating a younger man? Sure it works for Demi and Ashton, but when you travel in private jets and have a staff of ten to attend to your every whim, why shouldn't it work?

In order to examine this ever-growing phenomenon, we interviewed Kelly Koran, an attractive strawberry blonde who hangs out at Jillsy's Bar and Grill in downtown Seattle. Kelly had a lot to tell us about the younger man/older woman scene.

In Kelly's own words:

Hi! Is the tape rolling? My name's Kelly.

I guess you could call me a modern woman of the twenty-first century. I have a platinum gold card, lots of sexy underwear, my own Web site, and I make a good living on eBay.

Excuse me. Tom? I'll have another Dewar's on the rocks, double, okay?

Where was I? Oh, yeah, about me. I've always prided myself on my openness. People will say to me, "Kelly, I love the color of your hair. Is it natural?"

"Natural? Sure!" I reply. "For seventy-five bucks, you can have natural, too!" [Laughter, quite loud]

Now, about my age I'm scrupulously honest. I'm thirty-nine and proud of it. I'm the best I can be. I've learned to like myself. I've learned to like scotch. [Laughter] *No, seriously, though. I'm so much more together than I was in my twenties.*

The way things are today, I'd never want to be a teenager again.

Hey! I'm not getting older, I'm getting richer. In fact, I've got all the money I'll ever need, if I die by four o'clock. [Laughter]

Tom? Another round for me and the reporter, here. No?
Okay, just me then.

Okay, now you were asking about younger men? Listen, last week,
across this very same crowded bar stool, I met a gorgeous guy. Gor-
geous? I swear he was a young Colin Farrell. Really, fabulous. And the
buns on him! We get to talking, you know, kind of flirting like, and after
a couple of beers, he mentions he's twenty-seven years old.

Good God, I think to myself.

"Good gracious," I say to him, "you're a baby!"

"No way," he says, "I'm not that much younger than you."

Now, my best friend, Cindy, is sitting right next to me, and Cindy says,
"Yeah, that's true, Kelly's only thirty-one." I smiled and didn't correct
her.

"You see what I mean?" says this fabulous hunk. "You ain't
so much older."

So I'd really done it. I'd lied about my age. Well, I kind of thought lying
would help to, you know, cement things between me and Mr. Twenty-
seven. [Deep sigh] *It didn't.*[1]

I don't really think lying about your age ever helps a
relationship . . . although sometimes it makes for a really interesting
one-night stand. [Laughter]

Well, you get my drift, right? So, how old are you? Yeah? That's great.
Twenty-four's great. Umm. Double dozens.

The French, you know, they say by the time a woman's forty, she gets the
face she deserves. So, what'd you think? I got the face I deserve? No,
don't answer that, I'm only kidding. I ain't near forty yet.

Tom? One more.

[Loud gulping, ice cubes rattling]

Hell, what do the French know, anyway. Am I right? Or what? I mean,
they don't even use deodorant. How smart can they be?

---

1. For a more detailed explanation see Sex on the First Date, page 78.

MANHATTAN COCKTAIL

Directed by
DOROTHY ARZNER
Story by
ERNEST VAJDA
Screen play by
ETHEL DOHERTY

WITH
NANCY CARROLL
RICHARD ARLEN
and PAUL LUKAS

a Paramount Picture

Anyway, I came to the conclusion it's probably better to be honest about your age. Like honesty's the best policy and all that stuff.

All the movie stars, you know, they all date younger men and no one bats an eyelash. Like for instance, Demi Moore's like forty-one and Ashton is what, like twenty-five? Mira Sorvino, she's thirty-six and she just married a guy who is twenty-three!! Cameron Diaz is like ten years older than Justin Timberlake. Hey, I know what I'm talking about here because I read **People** *magazine every week.*

You know, Kathleen Turner, that actress from **Body Heat,** *I read in some article her husband said to her, "I may not know everything in the world about sex, but I know what you like." Isn't that just the most romantic thing you've ever heard? [Sigh]*

But the point is, all this makes me wonder, you know, is this a trend or what? Are there only twenty-year-old men in Hollywood?

My friend Cindy says all the forty-year-old guys are dating eighteen-year-olds.

Cindy should know, she dated a younger guy—and I mean, younger— for a real long time, until the day he found her Erno Laszlo black soap in the bathroom and said, "My mom uses this." Poor Cindy discovered she was only five years younger than Mikey's mother.

Jeez, his mother!

I gotta have another drink; just thinking about that's downright depressing. Come on, Tom, set 'em up, my friend. Don't this joint have the cutest bartenders? Tommy, hey, Tommy, come here, yeah, over here. What time you off tonight? Oh. How about tomorrow?

Yeah, well, actually, I'm busy, too. I just forgot. [Laughter] I mean, I have this thing. No, really, don't worry about it. Listen, I think I'll switch to brandy, okay? Thanks. [Long exhale]

You know, I'd really, really like to have a few words with the joker who said, "You're not getting older, you're getting better."

Better? Okay bub, I'd say to him, I'll tell you what's better: my eggplant parmigiana and my relationship with my shrink.

Wanna know what's worse? My gums, my fear of catching some fatal sex disease, my skin tone, my visits to the gynecologist, my upper arms, my eyes. I can't read a blessed thing anymore without my damn glasses. And, I'm not even going to mention my thighs.

Better? Better, my ass.

Jus' make me twenty-three again, for jus' one more decade, and I'll show you better.

But, no, we aren't allowed to turn back the clock, are we? No siree, bob. We make the teensy-weensy mistake of getting a little older and we're stuck with it forever.

The truth is: I'm Not Getting Older, I'm Getting OLDER!!!!

[Weeping obscures the next couple of sentences on the tape.]

Say, ya know, you're a very nice person, so I'm gonna tell ya something. I made a big decision. In my next life I'm coming back as Tina Turner— then it won't matter how old I get, I'll always have great legs.

'Scuse me, but I think I'm gonna be sick. Cindy, help me to the ladies', would ya?

Kelly's story teaches us many lessons. First and foremost, of course, that drinking and interviewing don't mix. Second, that lying about your age probably doesn't help a relationship.

We also see that Kelly is not particularly pleased about getting older.

What about you?

Are you currently dating a man who's too young for you?

This is difficult to determine because everyone always says, "Age is relative." Everyone over thirty, that is.

An easy test, however, can demonstrate whether or not your current lover is too young for you. Simply answer the following four questions:

   1. Is his idea for a great date:

      a. a movie and dinner

      b. playing video games

2. When his mother calls, does she say:
   a. "When are you coming to dinner?"
   b. "Make sure my son wears his raincoat today."

3. Is his favorite make-out music:
   a. Ray Charles
   b. Nine Inch Nails

4. Does he think hip-hop is:
   a. cool
   b. oldies music

If you answered (a) to most of these questions, then you are in just the right age group. If you answered (b), then perhaps you might want to consider any of the following four procedures: plastic surgery, liposuction, collagen shots, and Botox.

After all, if it's good enough for Demi, why not you?

dating married men

Sooner or later in the dating process, every unattached female is bound to encounter, date, and fall in love with a married man. Among single women, it is said that falling in love with a married man is as inevitable as Michael Jackson needing a lawyer.

In 1982, Yves Montand, the gorgeous Italian actor, explained to *People* magazine why there are so many married men on the dating market. "I think a man can have two, maybe three affairs while he is married," Yves said, without flinching, "But three is the absolute maximum. After that you are cheating."

There was no comment from Mrs. Montand.

We know that women have dated married men for centuries, but it was not until the publication of *Sex and the Single Girl* that the practice of adultery was both sanctioned and encouraged. Written with the same editorial integrity that Helen Gurley Brown would later employ when establishing *Cosmopolitan* magazine, *Sex and the Single Girl* formulated the then scandalous thesis that (a) it was okay for single girls to sleep with married men and (b) it was even better if the girls enjoyed it!

Critics argued there was a basic misconception at the heart of this book. While *Sex and the Single Girl* promised to "explode the myth that a girl must be married to enjoy a satisfying life," in the very first sentence of the book, Helen Gurley Brown boasted of being married to the man of her dreams, owning two Mercedes-Benzes, and having a full-time maid. If the single life was so great, argued some critics, why did Mrs. Brown feel compelled to let us know she was no longer dateless and desperate?

"She's got no right to preach to single gals," wrote a thirty-four-year-old single gal from Hackensack, New Jersey. "I

Warner Bros. present

BETTE DAVIS

MARKED WOMAN

HUMPHREY BOGART

LOLA LANE · ISABEL JEWELL · EDUARDO CIANNELLI
JANE BRYAN · ROSALIND MARQUIS · MAYO METHOT
ALLEN JENKINS · JOHN LITEL · BEN WELDEN · HENRY O'NEILL
Directed by LLOYD BACON — *Music and Lyrics by Harry Warren & Al Dubin*
A FIRST NATIONAL PICTURE

don't take advice from my married sister. Why should I listen to this Gurley dame?"

Yet despite such attacks, Mrs. Brown surely struck a resonant chord when she described the reasons why single gals are more attractive to men than married ladies are. Here is where the author reveals a genuine gift for translating complex intellectual and psychological motivations into a language that any layperson can easily grasp. "She [the single gal] has more time and often more money to spend on herself. She has the extra twenty minutes to exercise every day, an hour to make up her face for their date. She has all day Saturday to whip up a silly, wonderful cotton brocade tea coat—or hours to find it at a bargain sale—to entertain him in the next day."

As if this insight wasn't enough, the author continues to astound the reader by providing the kind of advice that only someone of Mrs. Brown's stature is qualified to give.

"As for cooking for married men, that's sheer insanity!" advises Mrs. Brown. "One reason you see them is to add glamour to your life. Once in a while you may honor a married man with a dinner invitation, or let's put it this way: if he comes trooping over with two mallard ducks he shot especially for you and a bottle of Cordon Bleu, cook his dinner."

Is it any wonder that *Sex and the Single Girl* was an enormous bestseller? Never before had any book explained in such detail the etiquette involved when our gentlemen callers tossed us a couple of bloody duck corpses. It was so reassuring to finally understand the proper method of handling this potentially embarrassing situation, especially since it comes up so often in the life of a single gal!

In general, the practice of dating married men has increased substantially since the days of Mrs. Brown. (We have to wonder if anyone is dating Mr. Brown and, if so, what does Mrs. Brown have to say about that?)

The reasons for the rise in dating married men is best explained by Ms. Mavis Davis, president of the Are You a Fabulous Single Person? dating agency of Oklahoma City, which specializes in arranging S&M (Singles and Marrieds) dates.

"There are more single gals around and not nearly enough men," says Ms. Davis, "so we have to borrow from the married pool to fill in the shortage.

"Besides, single gals, like myself, enjoy dating married men because there's a great deal of stability in the relationship," explains Ms. Davis. "You always know where you stand with a married man—directly behind the proverbial eight ball.

"The adulterous relationship has many other benefits as well. For example, it helps cement our feelings of insecurity and abandonment. At the same time, an affair with a married man reinforces what our moms always told us: no one will ever love us like our mothers. Actually, the joke is that married men love us *exactly* like our mothers in that they allow us no control over the relationship and require us to constantly tell them how great they are!"

Ms. Davis is herself currently involved in a ten-year relationship with a married man whose identity she refused to reveal. "His last name is Hucklestratmeyerhaus and his family lives in Wilbur, Oklahoma, on Jonestown Street," she said, "but that's *all* I'll tell you."

In promoting her dating agency, Ms. Davis recently published a pamphlet promoting the advantages of the S&M relationship. Entitled *Do You Enjoy Afternoon Sex?*, the book is given free of charge to all clients of the agency. In it, Ms. Davis explains the many advantages of dating a married man. For example:

You'll never have to be nice to his mother.

You'll always have a substantial excuse for your depression, lethargy, neurosis, and/or extra ten pounds.

You'll have lots of free time on the weekends and during Christmas vacation to shop, see your family, help the homeless, and feel rejected.

Running off to a hotel during lunch hour is a great way to stick to your diet.

You'll have a good reason to cry at movies.

You're in the glamorous company of such monumental love affairs as Tracy and Hepburn.

You don't have to deal with his dental appointments or laundry.

You don't have to pretend to be interested in his children.

You'll always miss him and he'll always be beholden to you, so the sex will usually be good, if not great.

You never have to attend funerals of his relatives or his family dinners.

You'll get plenty of practice delivering ultimatums. (See Ultimatums and Their Relationship to Holding Grudges, page 134.)

Once you agree to date married men, you quadruple your odds of getting a date.

"All in all, it's not such a bad deal," adds Ms. Davis. "You're relieved from many of the monotonous chores of matrimony and, very often, married men will pay your shrink bills. And, of course, you never have to worry that he'll divorce you. That beats sitting home and watching reruns of *Seinfeld*, doesn't it?"

breaking up and

breaking down

Love never dies of starvation,
but often of indigestion.

NINON DE LENCLOS,
1870

Your life should be filled with lawyers!

YIDDISH CURSE

Who's Virginia?

ROSE KENNEDY, WHEN ASKED WHY HER
DAUGHTER-IN-LAW JOAN LIVED IN BOSTON
WHILE HER SON TED LIVED IN VIRGINIA.

ultimatums
and their relationship to holding grudges

In the logical sequence of dating events, the first date leads to sex and then turns into the dreaded state called a relationship. The length of the formal relationship period is dependent upon many factors, including ex-girlfriends, commitment phobias, and the frequency of oral sex. Nonetheless, it almost always culminates in the process known as the ultimatum.

As is true for many traditional dating rituals, the ultimatum encounter is usually witless, degrading, and almost touchingly absurd.

Like neurosurgery, delivering the ultimatum is the most delicate of all procedures and needs to be handled very, very carefully in order to prevent irreparable ego scarring and loss of bladder control.

At the end of such an encounter, the single woman is either engaged or, most likely, hysterically dateless again.

Because there is such a great risk involved when employing the ultimatum, many women delay this stage, sometimes for months, sometimes for years, and sometimes until they can no longer remember why they wanted him in the first place.

This dilemma often motivates single women to seek psychiatric help. In fact, psychiatrists report that the two most often asked questions by single women when beginning therapy are:

1. How can I get the courage to deliver an ultimatum to my boyfriend?
2. How much do you charge for a session?

The answer to the ultimatum question, like so many answers you'll receive from your therapist, is quite simply: "How do you feel about that?"

(You can calculate your therapist's fee by using the following formula: Think of the most outrageous amount of money a person could conceivably charge for listening to you talk for forty minutes. Then multiply that figure by fifteen.)

how to deliver an ultimatum

It is a well-documented fact that the ultimatum comes up most often in relationships between single women and married men. During these affairs, women really get an opportunity to hone their ultimatum delivery technique, which will prove very useful later in life when (and if) these women ever become mothers. (No one on earth is better at delivering an ultimatum than a mother.)

Timing is everything when delivering an ultimatum. You must find that exact moment when your guy still believes that he is going to die of love for you, right before another woman comes along and interrupts him.

Single women dating single men can learn a lot about the fine art of delivering the ultimatum by studying the two most common procedures employed when delivering an ultimatum to a married man.

First, there is the technique known as the Ultimatum Retrieved (UR), which is when the ultimatum is delivered but not enforced. The following conversation between a married man and a single woman is an excellent example of the UR.

SHE: "Marry me, or else!"
HE: "Or else, what?"
SHE: "Or else, I'm going out with Herb in accounting."
HE: "You couldn't do that to me." (Optional: Voice breaks)
SHE: "Please, don't cry."
HE: "You won't go out with Herb?"
SHE: "No, I suppose not."
HE: "Great. How about Mexican for dinner?"

The UR, in its various disguises, can continue for years and years, long after Herb has left the accounting department.

The Counter Ultimatum (CU) is a more sophisticated technique for silencing the threat of the initial ultimatum and is apparent in an exchange such as:

SHE: "Marry me or I'll kill myself."
HE: "If you kill yourself, I'll kill myself."
SHE: "Really?"
HE: "I couldn't live without you. Don't you know that, kitten?"
SHE: "I guess I do."
HE: "Great. How about Mexican for dinner?"

In both of these cases, the married man neutralizes the ultimatum and thus buys himself more time. Eventually, however, the ultimatum is delivered once too often and the relationship splits apart. This is followed by a long period of tears and recriminations.

While this is a very difficult period, it is not without its advantages. It is during this time that women can work on their capacity to develop and cultivate a grudge.

how to hold a grudge

Of course, we know that some people are quick to forgive; they're basically decent and kind. They don't like confrontation, and they keep their temper and their complaints to themselves. They have learned the fine art of turning the other cheek. They would never try to steal your boyfriend. They do not think of suing if they slip on your bathroom mat. They never let their answering machines pick up a call when they are home. These people are not properly adjusted to life in the 2000s and should be avoided at all costs. It's only a matter of time before these people become hopelessly addicted to *Everybody Loves Raymond* and Zoloft.

Modern times demand appropriate action, introspection, and self-absorption. You cannot function today without the proper defense mechanisms, such as holding a grudge.

How good you are at grudge maintenance will depend on the strength of two very specific personality traits: a long memory and a short temper.

A really good memory is most important. You will need to train your brain to function like a computer, to store every hurt, every slight—sometimes for years—until the collection can be used to the greatest advantage. Retrieval of this data is most appropriate during the course of a heated argument, when your adversary is most vulnerable. Then you can fling your well-aimed grievance for maximum effect.

Second, you need a short temper, which you will use both as an excuse to release your venom and as your explanation for being really mean, rotten, and selfish. (Actually, you do not need to think of yourself as being mean, rotten, and selfish as long as your mother continually accuses you of these shortcomings. Eventually, you will believe her.)

To strengthen your capacity to hold a grudge against a former lover, it is wise to practice with your immediate family. In general, scientists note that it's best to save your worst grudges for relatives. This is called keeping it in the family and is effective because you've known your family for a long time and are apt to have a history of complaints and lots of old wounds you can bring up at the crucial moment.

Just think, if you can develop a strong enough grudge against the majority of your relatives, you may never again have to attend another family get-together. Instead of driving two hours in traffic to spend another two hours arguing with your brother-in-law, you'll be able to spend the afternoon at home, watching a DVD and eating lots of junk food before dinner, peacefully ruining your appetite.

After those held against parents and siblings, the best grudges are those held against spouses, especially ex-spouses, with lovers and ex-lovers running a close second. Grudges stemming from family feuds, divorce settlements, jealousy, and unrequited love can be educational. After a nasty fight with your mother or a vicious plate-throwing evening with your future ex-boyfriend, you will be much better prepared for life in the office.

If you begin practicing young enough, it is possible to still be holding a grudge against your high school boyfriend while gleefully celebrating the birth of your first grandchild.

The great thing about holding a grudge is that you really do get better at it with age—and unlike innocence or happiness, it's truly one of those emotions that, with a little effort, will never desert you.

bad moods:
behavior for a new age

Experts agree that the 1990s were particularly difficult for the chronically cranky (known in psychological terms as Crankpots). Every time they turned around, Donald Trump had erected yet another co-op they would never be able to afford. Celebrities like Madonna and Courtney Love took the joy out of being famous. And, week after week, Crankpots were browbeaten by television shows featuring news-type stories about folks who enjoyed better lives, prettier houses, cuter children, firmer breasts, and friendlier pets. According to Canadian psychoanalyst and professional dog-walker Helga Freundly, "Many people spent the past decade in a bad mood. What a bummer, eh?"

Yes, it seemed a pretty grim decade until one Crankpot named Rhonda Sperling decided she was grumpier than hell and wasn't going to take it anymore. An inspiration to grudge holders and curmudgeons everywhere, Rhonda Sperling is one Crankpot who turned her life around.

Interviewed in her trailer in New Paltz, New York, Rhonda told a reporter for the hit television show *Entertainment Tonight and Every Night, Forever and Ever* how she had broken the gloom of the 1990s.

"Yeah, it was a pretty sour decade for me," Rhonda said as she stirred her instant coffee with a nail file, "I was hoping for great things in the nineties. Then I got left without a date for my stepbrother's wedding and threatened with a lawsuit when that idiot neighbor jogged into my snowmobile. It was only February and I was broke. Well, I was feeling pretty low, but then I'm rummaging through some back issues of *The National Enquirer* and I come across this story about an ex-lover of Rock Hudson's who sued the estate and won twenty-one million based on this concept of *mental anguish*.

"Hell, I think to myself, you want to talk mental anguish, come talk to me.

"So, I call Legal Aid and I'm referred to a lawyer who tells me I've got a really good case because of all I've suffered in my life. She says, 'Rhonda, you've had more mental anguish in your life than Elizabeth Taylor, J-Lo, and that skinny Olsen Twin combined.' And I know I'm on to something."

Rhonda Sperling wasted no time. Aided by her team of lawyers, she filed twenty-two separate lawsuits in the states of New York, New Jersey, and Connecticut, all on the grounds of mental anguish. A brief catalog includes litigation asking for the following settlements:

- $600,000 from Mrs. MacGregor, Rhonda's fourth-grade teacher, for not allowing Rhonda access to the little girls' room when she really, really needed it—as Rhonda later proved in front of the entire class.
- $450,000 from Mrs. Godley, Rhonda's sixth-grade teacher, for snickering when Rhonda accidentally called her "Mommy."
- $7,000,000 from David Zeller, who turned down Rhonda's invitation to be her date to the Junior Prom and, at the same time, asked if he could date Rhonda's sister, Nancy.
- $2,000,000 from Roger Risoto, who lived with Rhonda for six months after his divorce and then split for L.A. when Rhonda mentioned getting married.
- $3,000,000 from Joel Heinie, who broke up with Rhonda the day before New Year's Eve.
- $13,000,000 from Sam Carlucci, the love of Rhonda's life, who promised for six years to leave his wife, but didn't.
- $2,000 from Mr. Elliot, Rhonda's hairdresser, who cut Rhonda's bangs way too short.

- $75,000 from Kenny Craig, who promised to take Rhonda to the Bahamas but took his supposedly ex-girlfriend instead.
- $7,500 from Danny Kravitz, who, after dinner and the movies, asked if he could see Rhonda again but then never called.
- $150,000 from Howard Stern for subjecting Rhonda to his opinion one night while she was randomly switching channels on the radio.
- $6,000 from all the personnel managers who rejected Rhonda's application for employment.
- $750 from the postal employee who mislaid Rhonda's last welfare check.
- $2,000,000,000 from Rhonda's mother, just on general principle.

On the advice of her lawyers, Rhonda is also suing several groups of people. This puts Rhonda on the record books as the first person in America to file a class action suit for general mental anguish. She is hoping to win the following settlements:

- $2,000 from anyone on the planet born with a trust fund or inheritance.
- $65,000 from every guy in Fair Lawn High School, Class of 1986, who did not ask Rhonda to the Junior Prom.
- $47 from every woman in the world with no upper arm jiggle.
- $1,000 from every person who owns oceanfront property anywhere on the planet.
- $64 from every driver who ever cut off Rhonda's car on the freeway.
- $2,500 from every woman who is younger, prettier, and/or more successful than Rhonda.
- 25¢ from every panhandler who ever asked Rhonda for spare change.

Rhonda has been advised that, although her case(s) look very promising, she may be in litigation well into the year 2030.

"What do you think of that?" Rhonda says with a shrug. "The 2000s may not be so terrible after all."

the six stages
of dying from a broken heart

Can you actually die of a broken heart? Although a broken heart is only one chapter in the great Book of Love, it's an especially ugly one.

The actual process by which we recover from a broken heart has been studied in detail by Dr. Elaine Kahula-Rossi. An eminent psychotherapist specializing in obsessional behavior in San Francisco, Dr. Kahula-Rossi was on sabbatical for a year and living on a small island in the Puget Sound area near Seattle, Washington, when she accidentally became involved with several brokenhearted people.

During her early-morning walkies with her dog, Friskie, the doctor came upon several brokenhearted people who'd washed ashore during the night. Some of the people had drifted up from as far away as Los Angeles and San Diego.

The sight of these depressed, sunburnt, bloated people sparked the good doctor's curiosity. She began to study the effects of rejection and salt water, and wondered whether there was a pattern to the process of recovering from getting dumped.

Almost immediately, the doctor noted that although her patients had different ages, religions, and sexual preferences, all of them seemed to display similar characteristics. She closely observed these people and spent many hours listening to them discuss their former love objects, supplementing her personal observations with extensive research from watching reruns of *Friends* and *Frazier*.

Ultimately, Dr. Kahula-Rossi concluded there were five stages in the process of dying from a broken heart. A few years later, however, Dr. Kahula-Rossi added on a sixth stage in order to placate her patients who demanded an even half-dozen.

denial

The first stage is denial, where the patient refuses to acknowledge her pain. This stage is most often characterized by the twin expressions, "I never liked his hair anyway," and "He wasn't that good in bed, not really."

The patient in denial refuses to accept reality. "I'm sure he'll call tomorrow," patients will say again and again.

It is during denial that patients are most likely to believe one of the three most common myths of modern romance:

1. Single men want to be married.
2. Married men actually leave their wives.
3. Someday your prince will come.

The patient will fantasize that, if she only waits long enough, her love object will eventually apologize and say he's changed his mind; everything he said was all a mistake and now he realizes he's more in love than ever before. The patient imagines herself giving the love object a hard time, perhaps hanging up the phone, although, inevitably, she plans to both forgive him and to get an incredibly expensive gift out of the misunderstanding.

She fails to recognize that the modern man has so much heart that he apparently believes it is selfish to waste it all on one woman. "There are only two kinds of perfect men," writes the good doctor, "the dead and the deadly. But most women don't realize this until they are well into the geriatric years, when a bowl of vanilla ice cream is much more appealing than any man."

When the patient's fantasy of reconciliation fails to materialize, she often experiences a compulsive urge to call or write the love object's current girlfriend, wife, mother, boss, or lawyer, thus signaling a leap into the second stage.

anger and depression

Anger and depression (A&D) are the dual components of the second stage. Temper tantrums are frequent and violent, varying according to different individuals, although it is fairly safe to assume that all expensive china and credit cards should be hidden at this point in the patient's recovery.

During A&D, patients are prone to minor accidents, inflicting superficial damage to various limbs. Stubbed toes, black-and-blue marks, and razor nicks are frequent occurrences. Lost wallets and car keys are systematic. Patients often rediscover the head-banging techniques they originally employed at the age of twenty-seven months. It is best, at this stage, to discourage patients from operating moving vehicles or making major decisions about interior decorating. It is during A&D that women are drawn to wearing leopard prints, an unfortunate habit that can prove irreversible.

Once the anger subsides, depression usually sets in. The patient will feel that life without her love object is simply not worth living. If the patient begins gazing longingly at the kitchen stove or the medicine cabinet, it is wise to hire a twenty-four-hour nurse. During this stage the patient will either cry a lot, sleep eighteen or nineteen hours a day, or watch daytime television.

self-pity

The transition into stage three, which Dr. Kahula-Rossi calls the stage of self-pity, is so gradual that it's difficult to distinguish it from depression. Both are characterized by intense absorption in food and beverage. A weight gain of ten to fifteen pounds, or more, is not unusual at this transitional stage.

The major difference, however, is that during the self-pity period, the patient gradually becomes more verbal. While the depression stage is characterized by heavy, prolonged sighing, and the occasional hand-wringing, the self-pity stage sees the patient begin to speak again. Dr. Kahula-Rossi has noted that, while engaged in the self-pity stage, patients are particularly prone to ask rhetorical questions, such as: *Why does this always happen to me?* or *What's wrong with me?* or *I'm a good person, aren't I?*

Explaining this phenomenon, Dr. Kahula-Rossi has written, "It is my theory that since patients are totally self-involved at this stage, they feel quite justified in asking questions that only they, themselves, can answer."

At this stage, it doesn't really matter how you answer the patients' questions. If you agree with their morbid assessment of the world, they'll get sarcastic and say, "Well, you're a big help. I need you like a hole in the head." If you disagree with the patient, he or she will accuse you of patronizing him or her. Dr. Kahula-Rossi has concluded that patients must work through their own self-pity. "That's why it's called self-pity in the first place," notes the astute doctor.

stop feeling hurt

Ultimately, patients get past feeling self-pity when they let go of feeling hurt. They can do this either by falling in love with someone else, by being born-again, or by receiving a negative prognosis from a doctor. Any of these procedures have been known to give patients a new lease on life. However, barring these extremes, the patient may come out of the self-pity stage on her own accord.

Once patients let go of the hurt, they are prepared to fulfill the fifth and most satisfying stage of recovery. They stop concentrating on hurting themselves and start thinking about hurting someone else, namely the love object.

hurt someone else

During this stage, patients will become consumed with plans for revenge. They spend enormous amounts of time and energy concocting ways of making the ex-love object pay through the nose either emotionally or financially. If the couple was not married, it is during this stage that the woman begins asking about palimony.

A classic example of a patient successfully working through

the Hurt Someone Else stage is that of author Nora Ephron, who got the very best revenge by writing *Heartburn*, humiliating her ex-husband and making a bushel of money at the same time.

(Although they say living well is the best revenge, they're wrong. As any jilted woman will tell you, getting revenge is the best revenge.)

It is only after some kind of satisfaction is achieved that the patient can enter the sixth and final stage, recovery.

recovery

It is during this final stage that the patient frees herself from the pain of the past and her fear of the future. With the guidance and support of her therapist, the patient discovers she can go out into the world and start over.

"We try to project how long it'll take a patient to have their next heartbreak," confesses Dr. Kahula-Rossi. "Sometimes, we form a pool. Last week, for instance, I won four hundred and thirty-five dollars on one of my manic depressives who constantly falls for alcoholic artists."

Amazingly, the process of falling in love, getting dumped, and recovering from a broken heart can repeat itself throughout the patient's lifetime.

a Paramount Picture

PRODUCED BY FAMOUS PLAYERS-LASKY CORPORATION

ADOLPH ZUKOR AND JESSE L. LASKY
PRESENT

J. M. BARRIE'S

A Kiss for Cinderella

A HERBERT BRENON PRODUCTION
WITH

BETTY BRONSON,
TOM MOORE *and*
ESTHER RALSTON

SCREEN PLAY BY
WILLIS GOLDBECK and TOWNSEND MARTIN

Paramount
Pictures

FAMOUS PLAYERS-LASKY CORP.

how to wash that man out of your hair

without getting split ends

Okay, so the bum left you. He walked out. He's gone. He's history.

You feel bad. Real bad.

You want to know: Is there anything I can do to feel better? Anything, that is, that won't either add five inches to my hips or render me unconscious.

The answer is yes.

I know because I've successfully recovered from two major heartbreaks, one and a half minor infractions, and too many of the "Gosh-I-wish-this-would've-worked-out" variety to count.

Experts advise that speed is of the essence in getting over a heartbreaker. Prolonged misery and uninterrupted pining for lost love can result in nasty wrinkles and crow's feet that will severely depreciate your resale value on the open dating market.

Use the following guidelines to zip through the pain and heartache—fast—before your tail fins are outdated.

tip #1: say, "i should've married roger!"

The first thing I do in my own personal recovery program is to say out loud, "I should've married Roger."

Roger was the guy I dated after college. He was kind, considerate, polite, and never late for anything.

Roger enjoyed celebrating our anniversaries (the day we met, the night we first made love, our first visit to Bloomingdale's) with a bottle of Mateus rosé.

Roger was friendly to all my friends. He brought me flowers and mailed me lots of studio cards. He replaced my broken appliances.

One day he said, "You're the kind of woman who deserves to travel in a chauffeur-driven limousine."

I thought Roger was basically a nice, if somewhat lonely, guy. When I wasn't with him, I appreciated how well he treated me, but when we were together, I had a hard time concentrating and tended to forget almost everything he told me.

Even so, Roger was not discouraged. "I'm here for you," Roger would say to me. "I love you, and one of these days you'll feel the same way about me. You'll see."

He frequently talked about marriage.

So, naturally, I dumped Roger for a roadie I met one drunken night at a club on the Jersey shore.

Roger took it quite badly. He disappeared for almost thirty-six hours and was discovered wandering aimlessly across the George Washington Bridge.

I felt bad, but not as bad as I felt two weeks later when my roadie boyfriend drop-kicked me for a groupie with flaming red hair and a twenty-two-inch waist.

I told myself I had no regrets about the way things had worked out, although that was after I told myself, "I should've married Roger," which was about five seconds *after* my mother told me, "You should've married Roger, you numbskull!"

Yet, in truth, dumping Roger was not entirely masochistic on my part. I was never really attracted to him. In fact, when I think about Roger, the main physical characteristics I recall are the enormous amount of black hair on his back and his awful cologne. (When I tell myself I should've married Roger, I leave out the memories of waking up in the morning to sheets covered with hair and pillows reeking of English Leather.)

I think it's safe to assume that every woman has, or had, a

Roger in her life, that one really nice guy with a fatal flaw (or two) who was crazy about her.

So, fill in the blank and repeat after me, " I should've married _____ . "

Now, once you have the reassurance of knowing someone actually wanted to marry you, you can move on to more specific ways of getting over of the bum who didn't.

tip #2: get rid of everything that reminds you of him

Pack all of his things into one suitcase. Call this your "griefcase." Make sure you collect everything that reminds you of him—his toiletries, the mash notes he wrote, the seashells he collected for you at the beach, the portable television you bought for his promotion, the teddy bear he gave you for your birthday, his photographs, the matchbooks and ticket stubs you saved, the silverware and towels you stole from the motel where you spent your first date. Pack all these things—except for the television and any other electronic gifts, if they are still functional.

If there's not enough room for everything in your griefcase, use a "griefcarton" or, if necessary, a "grieftrunk." If you were living with or married to the bum, you may need a "griefvan."

tip #3: grieve

Spend the next twenty-four hours wallowing in your grief. Immerse yourself in memories of him.

- Play all the CDs and DVDs that remind you of him.
- Wear the sexy nightgown you bought for that weekend in the mountains.
- Mix up a pitcher of his favorite cocktails and reminisce about the last time you two got plastered together.
- Sort through every item in your griefcase. Read every one

of his notes, run your fingers over the embossing on his business card, sniffle over every movie ticket stub.

After thirteen or fourteen hours, you'll start to get restless and begin to wonder if the bum is worth all of your suffering. You will decide he is and cry for another hour and forty-five minutes.

You will consider suicide and then remember you haven't yet worn those fabulous red Manolo Blahnik high heels, so you still have something worth living for.

By the end of the twenty-four-hour period, you will undoubtedly have bored yourself to sleep.

tip #4: modify your behavior

After your day of grief isolation, you may be fooled into thinking you're over him for good. Be particularly careful, because, like any of your major addictions (alcohol, drugs, cigarettes, the Ice Capades), you can easily fall back into your destructive patterns.

Thus, you need to train yourself to refrain from thinking about him. Psychiatrists call this "behavior modification" and have used the basic technique to train laboratory rats, so, with a little effort, the method will work for you, too.

The procedure is simple: every time he comes into your mind, run into the kitchen and start chopping an onion.

Work furiously and be sure to keep your face close to the cutting board. (WARNING: Do not use any of those stupid onion-cutting tricks your mom taught you, such as running cold water or sticking a match between your lips.) Continue chopping for ten minutes or until you are crying too hard to see straight.

When you go out, you must take the onions, knife, and cutting board with you. Keep them in your purse, and, if you think about him while driving to the dentist, pull over to the side of the road and chop that onion!

If you punish yourself in this way, you will stop thinking about him well before your second pot of onion soup.

tip #5: learn to cope with the r.a.j.e. quartet

The R.A.J.E. Quartet is the term psychiatrists have coined to cover the four basic elements of a broken heart: revenge, anger, jealousy, and envy.

REVENGE

Revenge is the healthiest of these emotions and should be encouraged at all times. Spend a lot of time plotting your revenge. Even if you never actually slash his tires, toss rotten eggs at his front door, or leave obscene messages on his voice mail, it's still satisfying to contemplate these activities.

ANGER

Anger is a difficult emotion for all of us to handle. Working through our anger provides shrinks with a wellspring of material, along with working through our guilt over sex, which is another story altogether. As the noted psychiatrist Emil Kohutten has written, "If my patients didn't have such a profoundly difficult time handling their anger, I wouldn't get to drive a new BMW every year."

JEALOUSY

Jealousy is the one emotion that women are most accustomed to feeling. We are taught, almost from birth, to be jealous of our fellow females. From the first time we attempt to suffocate our newborn baby sister to five minutes ago when we gave serious consideration to tripping the thin blonde standing in front of us at the ATM, most women accept jealousy as a prerequisite to their daily lives.

The problem is that men are not nearly as suspicious as we are. A woman in love could easily be jealous of a store mannequin. I once spent an entire evening seething with jealousy when I saw a pair of hoop earrings on Brian's night table. It took me *two days* of silent suffering before I remembered that the earrings were mine.

Brian, on the other hand, could've found a pair of jockey shorts in my bedsheets and not given it a second thought. He believed that no woman on whom he bestowed his attentions could even think of any other man and, damn it to hell, he was right.

ENVY

Envy, the fourth and last of the Big Four emotions, is the feeling we most try to deny. We tell ourselves we do not envy anyone else's life, that we are entirely above the emotion.

This, of course, is a whopping big lie.

The truth is we are plagued with thoughts of envy and we strive mightily to evoke the emotion in others.

Consequently, the best way for us to deal with envy is to admit our feelings and accept them as part of who we are.

We can learn how to express our true self by taking a lesson from the world's most legendary heroine when she said, "Oh, Rhett, everyone will be pea green when they see our house . . . I want everyone who's been mean to me to feel bad."

Right on, Miss Scarlett!

tip #6: getting rid of split ends

So, now you've dealt with revenge, anger, jealousy, and envy; you've reminded yourself of all the men who really wanted you (okay, the *man* who really wanted you); you've disposed of all your ex's briefs and other paraphernalia; you've grieved your little heart out; you've changed your pattern of behavior; and you've brushed up on *Gone With the Wind*. In short, you've taken all the steps required to wash that man out of your hair, permanently. Now you are ready to embark, once more, on the road to romance.

Close this book. Take a deep breath.

Open this book to the section How to Call a Man for a Date, page 66. Begin, again.

Oh, and as for those troublesome split ends. Darling, you treat damaged hair in the same way you treat damaged men. You cut your losses.

Move on to your next fabulous haircut—and your next fantastic man!

"STAND UP and CHEER!"
with
WARNER
BAXTER
MADGE EVANS
SYLVIA FROOS
JOHN BOLE
JAMES DUN
"AUNT JEMIN
SHIRLEY TEM
ARTHUR BY
RALPH MO
NIGEL B
"SKINS" M
LUCIEN LIT
NICK
MITCHEL
STEPI
Produced by
WINFIELD SHEEHAN
Associate Producer and
Collaborator on Story & Dialogue
LEW BROWN

afterword

The poor wish to be rich, the
rich wish to be happy, the single
want to be married, and the
married wish to be dead.

ANN LANDERS,
PEOPLE,
NOVEMBER 24, 1986

For three days after death, hair
and fingernails continue to grow,
but the phone calls taper off.

JOHNNY CARSON

dating revisited

As I mentioned in the Preface, I began writing this book shortly after getting unceremoniously dumped by Jim.

That was six months ago. At about the same time, I had lunch with my friend, Lisa. Over margaritas, I told Lisa the whole miserable story.

"That schmuck!" said Lisa. "What guy in his right mind would do that to you? Listen, I guarantee, you haven't heard the last from this bozo. He'll call again, you'll see, to tell you he's made a big mistake."

"Gee, Lisa, I don't know."

"Listen to me, I *know* about these things. I've seen it happen a million times. Guys are so dense. One day, when you're least expecting it, Jim'll call to say he's picked the wrong woman."

"He said this other woman was a doctor."

"Doctor, schmoctor. A bestselling author beats a stupid MD any day."

"He said they met online. In a chat room, no less."

"Okay, so they've had a romantic beginning; that doesn't mean he won't come to his senses. He'll call and beg you to forgive him. Just give him another chance. He'll whine like mad about going crazy if you two don't get back together again."

"You think?" I said, rather enjoying the image in my mind of Jim on his knees.

"Absolutely," said Lisa. "And it'll be great for your self-esteem when you tell him to screw off."

"Do I have to be so . . . abrupt?"

"You wouldn't actually want to see that slime bucket again, would you?"

"Well . . ."

"Where's your self-respect? Of course you wouldn't want to see him again."

"No, I suppose not."

"Right."

Well, four months have gone by, and here I am, at the end of this book that I'd hoped to conclude with an account of Jim's phone call. The problem is that Jim hasn't called.

Lisa says not to worry. "The longer he waits to call, the bigger a jerk he is. When a guy is really, really stupid it takes him longer to figure out his mistakes. Maybe six months, maybe a year. If this guy's a real boob, it may take a couple of years, but you'll see, he'll call. Eventually."

"Are you sure?"

"You know something, sweetie? If he doesn't call, it only means one thing. He's not even man enough to admit his mistakes."

For obvious reasons, I enjoy my talks with Lisa and have come to depend on her more and more since the "Jim Incident." We talk on the phone at least once a week, and tonight we're going to the movies together.

During the Coming Attractions, we'll eat popcorn and trash Jim. After the movie, we'll go out to dinner and discuss my feelings about Jim in greater detail, which, as always, will help deepen my understanding that boyfriends may come and go, but friends like Lisa are available on Saturday night.

> Linda Sunshine
> Saturday night in June
> New York City

the lexicon of love appendix

For all of you who wish that men came with a guidebook (or at least a decoder ring), here are some of the key phrases in the language of Love—as interpreted by each of the sexes—and a dictionary for surviving dating in the 2000s.

Word	BUSY
Use in a Sentence	I'm *busy* tonight.
Woman's Definition	I'm doing laundry but I want him to think I have a date.
Man's Definition	I have a date.
Word	COMMITMENT
Use in a Sentence	Yes, we have a *commitment* to each other.
Woman's Definition	I won't look at another man.
Man's Definition	I won't talk about other women.
Word	COMMON BOND
Use in a Sentence	We have a *common bond.*
Woman's Definition	We have mutual interests.
Man's Definition	She likes baseball.
Word	DATING
Use in a Sentence	I'm *dating* someone new.
Woman's Definition	I'm in the process leading to a relationship.
Man's Definition	I'm in the process of avoiding a relationship.

Word	FEELINGS
Use in a Sentence	In ANY context.
Woman's Definition	A topic for discussion.
Man's Definition	A really bad song.
Word	FRIENDS
Use in a Sentence	Let's be *friends*.
Woman's Definition	We can have dinner but no sex.
Man's Definition	We can have sex but we won't discuss our relationship.
Word	GREAT DATE
Use in a Sentence	I had a *great date* last night.
Woman's Definition	Flowers, nice restaurant, dancing, moonlit walk, conversation.
Man's Definition	Home-cooked meal at her place. Video games. Blow job.
Word	GUYS
Use in a Sentence	He says, "I'm meeting the *guys* for a drink."
Woman's Definition	He's going to pick up women.
Man's Definition	I'm meeting the guys for a drink and to pick up women.
Word	HONESTY
Use in a Sentence	Our relationship is based on *honesty*.
Woman's Definition	We're completely truthful with each other.
Man's Definition	Duh?

3- 2/2/06

Word	MARRIAGE
Use in a Sentence	I don't believe in *marriage*.
Woman's Definition	I'll change my mind when I meet the right guy.
Man's Definition	I don't believe in marriage.
Word	RELATIONSHIP
Use in a Sentence	Let's discuss our *relationship*.
Woman's Definition	Two people who've had more than three dates.
Man's Definition	An arrangement that will destroy my manhood.
Word	SOON
Use in a Sentence	I'll call you *soon*.
Woman's Definition	Two to three days, tops.
Man's Definition	Two weeks to never.
Word	WHITE LIE
Use in a Sentence	He says, "It was only a *white lie*."
Woman's Definition	He lied.
Man's Definition	I lied but it didn't count.